A collection of recipes from members of The Toronto Symphony,
famous guest artists and friends, compiled and written
by members of The Toronto Symphony Women's Committee

Edited by Ruth Koretsky
Designed by Frances Neish
Illustrated by Audrey Pratt

The Toronto Symphony Women's Committee
215 Victoria Street
Toronto, Ontario M5B 1V1

First Printing
August, 1980

Printed by
Pro-Art Graphics Ltd.

Co-ordinated and Typeset by
Concorde Consultants

Produced by
AdVenture Advertising

ISBN 0-9690447-0-4

The French call the conductor *chef d'orchestre*. This is admittedly rather a flimsy qualification for writing a preface to The Toronto Symphony Cookbook, so I will immediately add another much more potent one: I have put on about twenty pounds since I came to Toronto.

In November, 1978, my house was invaded by the whole orchestra for a party for which they brought the food — the quantity, quality, and variety of foods were all so staggering that I wondered for a moment whether we shouldn't just disband the orchestra and open up a chain of gourmet restaurants! The subtleties of dynamics, colour, and texture for which our orchestra is becoming increasingly renowned were all mirrored gastronomically that evening; now we offer you the opportunity to recreate this splendid profusion. The prowess of our great players as cooks was surpassed then only by their prowess as eaters. What higher recommendation could you look for!

Andrew Davis
Music Director

ACKNOWLEDGEMENT

Our thanks without measure go to all those food lovers and generous spirits whose contributions made this unique cookbook possible:

Present and past orchestra members
Guest artists
Friends of The Toronto Symphony
Staff of The Toronto Symphony

The Toronto Symphony Women's Committee

TABLE OF CONTENTS

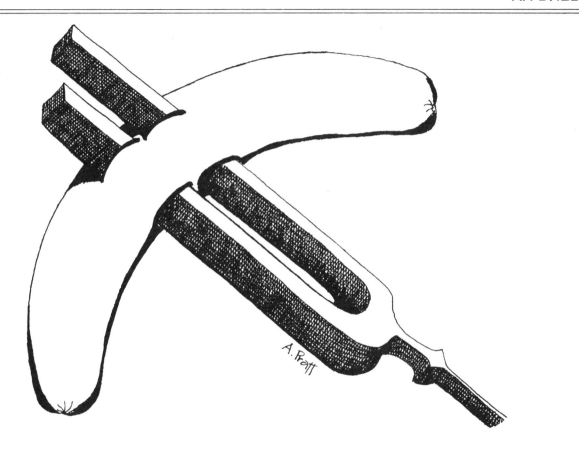

Serves 6 - 8

¼ cup	olive oil	1 10-oz.	can sliced mushrooms
2	carrots	5 oz.	ketchup
2	onions		Worcestershire sauce to taste
1 10-oz.	can tomato paste	1 tsp.	each of salt, pepper, oregano,
1 14-oz.	can wax beans, diced		basil, and garlic salt, or to taste
1	small jar sweet mixed pickles	2 7-oz.	cans flaked tuna, drained
1	small jar stuffed olives, cut up		

1. Dice carrots and parboil for a few minutes.
2. Fry chopped onions in oil.
3. In a large bowl mix together tomato paste, beans, diced sweet pickle, chopped olives, and chopped mushrooms. Add drained carrots, onions, and oil.
4. In a separate bowl, mix together ketchup, Worcestershire sauce, herbs, and seasonings, and add the two cans of flaked tuna.
5. Combine contents of both bowls. Mix well.

   Serve as a dip with toast points or crackers.

Ruth Budd carries her love of music to school children of all ages through the Community Education Programs, a project of The Toronto Symphony Women's Committee. She also appears on the popular children's T.V. show "Polka Dot Door". She is co-founder of a music school on the Cape Croker Indian Reservation.

"My Antipasto is one of my favourite recipes," says Ruth, "because it can be made in advance and refrigerated."

RUTH BUDD
Double Bass

Serves 8 - 10

2	whole chicken breasts		1	lemon, rind and juice
1 lb.	lean pork		½ tsp.	salt
2	chicken livers		pinch	pepper
6	stuffed olives, sliced		1 Tblsp.	dried sage
2	onions		1 can	beef broth or consommé
2	cloves garlic, crushed		2 Tblsp.	dry vermouth
2 Tblsp.	parsley		1	package gelatin
1	egg			

1. Set oven to 350° F.
2. Cut chicken breasts into strips.
3. Mince pork with chicken livers, onions, garlic, and chopped parsley. Add beaten egg, juice and grated rind of lemon, and seasonings.
4. Place half of this mixture in 9 x 5-inch loaf pan. Cover with chicken strips and the stuffed olives arranged in lines. Cover with remaining pork mixture.
5. Cover with foil and stand in a roaster half-filled with water. Bake for 2 hours in preheated oven.
6. Refrigerate overnight with heavy weights placed on top.
7. Next day place broth or consommé in pan with vermouth. Dissolve gelatin in this mixture over gentle heat. When dissolved and cooled, pour around the terrine. Refrigerate overnight. Unmould and cut into thin slices.

"Cooking is my hobby," says violinist Corol McCartney, and husband Stanley, former Co-Principal Clarinet in the orchestra, agrees. Their favourite style of entertaining is at small formal gatherings with an occasional large buffet on holidays. Both are from the West Coast and played with the Vancouver and Victoria symphonies before joining the TS in 1956.

COROL McCARTNEY
Violin

Serves 4

	12 squid, 3-4 inches long (body length)		

Stuffing:

1	can anchovy fillets, mashed	2	eggs
1	clove garlic, mashed	½ cup	fresh bread crumbs
2 Tblsp.	chopped parsley		freshly ground black pepper
1 tsp.	prepared Dijon mustard	1 tsp.	olive oil
2 Tblsp.	Parmesan cheese	1 tsp.	capers, mashed (optional)

1. Clean and skin squid.
2. Chop the tentacles finely and make stuffing with the above ingredients.
3. Place a bit of stuffing in each of the bodies of the squid.
4. Sprinkle squid with olive oil and place under broiler, turning several times until they are a rich, golden brown, about 15 minutes.

   Serve with lemon wedges.

During her years with The Toronto Symphony NanciCarole (Corkie) Monohan gained a reputation as one of its finest cooks. Her dishes are great favourites with members of the orchestra. Her recipes are unusual, original, and worth every effort involved in their preparation.

Corkie left the orchestra after the 1978 season, and is now a freelance double bass player, still frequently seen in TS concerts when additional players are needed.

NANCICAROLE (Corkie) MONOHAN
Double Bass

Serves 10 - 12

2 8-oz.	jars herring marinated in wine sauce	1		large green pepper, seeded and diced
1	coarsely chopped Spanish onion	1	16-oz.	bottle chili sauce

1. Drain herring and the few onions in the jars in a colander and rinse with cold water.
2. Toss in a bowl with other ingredients.
3. Marinate overnight and serve chilled with crackers.

Of Russian descent, Josef Sera was born in Winnipeg, where his recipe for Herring Salad originated. After studying in England at the Royal Academy of Music, he returned to play in the Winnipeg Symphony Orchestra. In 1946, he joined The Toronto Symphony and has been involved in teaching, chamber music, radio and television work, as well as recordings.

JOSEF SERA
Assistant Principal, 2nd Violins

Serves 8   A Russian Herring Appetizer

1½	Schmaltz herring (Remove the bones.) or 1 can sliced Schmaltz herring, boned	1 10-oz.	can sliced potatoes, chopped, or 2 - 3 medium potatoes, boiled and chopped
1	medium onion, sliced	2	hard-boiled eggs, chopped
1 19-oz.	can marinated beets, finely chopped	6 Tblsp.	mayonnaise

1. Cover bottom of a shallow salad bowl with thin slices of herring.
2. Cover this with onion rings.
3. Add half of the beets.
4. Add potatoes.
5. Cover with chopped eggs.
6. Add remaining beets.
7. Spread mayonnaise on top.
8. Refrigerate for 3 - 4 hours.

Violinist Yaakov Geringas and his pianist wife, Marina, have been in Canada since 1975, the year he joined The Toronto Symphony. Born in the former Lithuania, Yaakov graduated from the Vilna Conservatory, moved to Riga and became a member of the Philharmonic Chamber Orchestra, performing also as soloist in Riga and other cities in Latvia, Lithuania, and the U.S.S.R. "I have been teaching all my life," he says, "and at present am on the faculty of the Royal Conservatory of Music".

YAAKOV GERINGAS
Violin

chilled consommé
sherry
sour cream

Boston lettuce
caviar, black or red
lemon

For each serving:

1. Put 4 oz. chilled consommé and 1 Tblsp. sherry in the bottom of an 8-oz. wine glass.
2. Put 2 - 3 oz. sour cream on top of consommé.
3. Float a piece of Boston lettuce on sour cream.
4. Put 1 - 2 tsp. caviar on top of lettuce.
5. Squeeze some lemon juice on caviar and garnish with a slice of lemon on the side.
6. Refrigerate until serving time.

WILLIAM FINDLAY
Violoncello

Serves 6 - 8

20	large mushrooms	1 tsp.	salt
¾ cup	butter	½ tsp.	oregano leaves
1 cup	fresh onion, minced	1 cup	dried bread crumbs
5	medium garlic cloves, minced	½ cup	grated Parmesan cheese
½ cup	chopped parsley		

1. Clean mushrooms, remove and chop stems.
2. Melt butter; add onion, garlic, parsley, salt, oregano, and mushroom stems, and cook over low heat for 5 minutes.
3. Stir in dried bread crumbs and Parmesan cheese.
4. Spoon into mushroom caps.
5. Place under pre-heated broiler and broil for about 8 minutes, until tops are brown and mushrooms still crunchy.

Bassoonist Christopher Weait's recipes reflect his joy in cooking as well as his eclectic taste. He and his cellist wife have English backgrounds, and some of his recipes came from their families in England.

Busy with music education programs and chamber music, Christopher is also a popular recitalist.

CHRISTOPHER WEAIT
Co-Principal Bassoon

Serves 6 - 8 as an appetizer

2 - 3 Tblsp.	olive or vegetable oil
1	medium eggplant, cubed
1	medium onion, chopped
2	medium tomatoes, finely chopped

1	slice of caraway seed rye bread soaked in
3 Tblsp.	wine vinegar
1 tsp.	sugar

1. Sauté eggplant and onion in oil until soft. (Use only enough oil to coat the eggplant lightly.)
2. Combine with other ingredients in a bowl.
3. Chop until mixture is thoroughly blended and a coarse texture.
4. Chill overnight before serving.

Serve as an appetizer with crackers or pita bread, or as a side dish.

Nora Shulman loves to cook. She also loves to play and teach the flute and take ballet lessons. Born in Los Angeles, she graduated from the California State University Music School and played with the Denver Symphony for two years before joining the TS in 1974.

NORA SHULMAN
Associate Principal Flute

Serves 6

1	very large zucchini, peeled and cubed (2 cups)
6 Tblsp.	olive oil
3	cloves garlic
2	onions, peeled and thinly sliced
½ cup	thinly sliced celery
4 Tblsp.	tomato sauce
1 Tblsp.	capers
1½ Tblsp.	sugar
2 Tblsp.	vinegar
1 Tblsp.	lemon juice
12	stuffed olives, halved
1 Tblsp.	chopped parsley
	salt and pepper to taste

1. Sauté zucchini in oil with garlic and onion.
2. Add celery, tomato sauce, capers, sugar, vinegar, lemon juice, olives, and parsley.
3. Add salt and pepper to taste.
4. Simmer covered for 15 minutes, stirring occasionally; chill and serve with rye bread.

COROL McCARTNEY
Violin

CURRY DIP

1 cup	cottage cheese		1 cup	minced carrots
1½ - 2 cups	mayonnaise		¼ cup	vinegar
½ cup	chopped green pepper		1 Tblsp.	curry powder, or to taste

1. Mix in a blender or food processor.

   Serve with vegetable sticks.

ROQUEFORT DIP

4 oz.	Roquefort cheese		3 tsp.	coarse ground pepper
1 pint	mayonnaise		1 cup	sour cream
1	clove garlic, crushed		½ cup	buttermilk
1 tsp.	chopped chives			

1. Crumble Roquefort cheese.
2. Add mayonnaise, garlic, chives, and pepper.
3. Mix in, but do not beat, sour cream and buttermilk.

SCOTT WILSON
Horn

Serves 4 - 5

1 or 2	avocados	1	clove garlic, crushed
1 cup	sour cream or mayonnaise	1	tomato, skinned and diced
¼ tsp.	Tabasco		salt to taste
1 Tblsp.	lemon juice		

1. Mash avocado.
2. Add sour cream, Tabasco, lemon juice, garlic, and mix well.
3. Fold in tomato.

This is a special treat to be put on Tacos (p. 86) or eaten with Tortilla Chips. Tequila with salt and lime, or Margueritas work well as pre-dinner libations.

Canadian Brass have been hailed as "The Marx Brothers of Brass" and "musicians anybody could love" because of their spirited comedy, versatility, and informal stage manner, combined with their musicianship. Their many concert engagements keep the five members constantly on the move, leaving them little time at home to do much cooking. All five have a weakness for Mexican food, though, and Ronald Romm, especially, likes making Tacos whenever his schedule permits.

CANADIAN BRASS
Ronald Romm, Trumpet　　　*Eugene Watts, Trombone*　　*Charles Daellenbach, Tuba*
Fred Mills, Trumpet　　　　*Graeme Page, French Horn*

Serves 4 - 6

	juice of 4 lemons		½ tsp.	garlic powder
1 cup	water		½ tsp.	salt
5	sprigs of parsley		1 cup	tachena paste

1. At least 2 - 3 hours before serving, put lemon juice and 1 cup water in blender or food processor.
2. Rinse parsley and cut into small pieces. Add to blender, or processor, and blend to chop thoroughly.
3. Add garlic powder and salt. Then gradually add the tachena paste, blending well until it is the consistency of thick gravy.
4. Refrigerate until served. Flavour improves with time, and it may be kept in the refrigerator 3 - 4 days.
5. To serve: In the centre of a medium-size plate, place ½ cup of tachena mixture. Then pour on top a few tablespoonsful of olive oil. Sprinkle with paprika and garnish with tomatoes, olives, and parsley. Serve pita bread, cut into 2-inch wedges, on the side. Guests can scoop up the tachena with the pita and should feel free to lick their fingers more or less continuously.

Daniel Domb has contributed a recipe representative of his native Israel. His cello teacher there and later in Paris was Tortelier. At the age of 21, as a pupil of Leonard Rose, Daniel received his Master's degree from the Juilliard School of Music in New York. A Rockefeller grant led to more study in California with Gregor Piatagorsky. Daniel joined The Toronto Symphony in 1974. In his busy life of performing and teaching, he manages to make time for his two pastimes — cooking and photography. His photographs of The Toronto Symphony's tour of China were published in Maclean's.

DANIEL DOMB
Principal Violoncello

OLIVE CHEESE BALLS

Serves 4 - 6

½ lb.	sharp Cheddar cheese, grated	dash	cayenne pepper
2 Tblsp.	soft butter	25	large stuffed olives (or use
½ cup	flour		smoked oysters, pickles, etc.)

1. Set oven to 400° F.
2. Beat cheese and butter in beater bowl. Add flour and cayenne and continue beating until well blended. It will be very thick.
3. Take about a tablespoonful of mixture and flatten in palm of hand; then wrap around olive, covering, but not too thickly.
4. Bake for 15 minutes on cookie sheet. Should be firm and crisp.

Serve warm.

Bassoonist Nicholas Kilburn and his wife, Susan, love planning dinner parties and cooking for them. They belong to a dining society in which each of five symphony couples takes turns entertaining at dinner. They have often served their Olive Cheese Balls and Salmon Pâté at these parties. Nicholas has a reputation as a superb vegetable chopper because of his agility with a knife, acquired through years of experience in cutting reeds for his bassoon. He has been playing with The Toronto Symphony since 1959, as well as recording extensively with the Toronto Woodwind Quintet of which he was a founding member.

NICHOLAS KILBURN
Co-Principal Bassoon

Serves about 20 for snack or with cocktails

1 1-lb.	can red salmon	
1 8-oz.	package cream cheese, softened	
1 Tblsp.	lemon juice	
2 tsp.	horseradish (thick part)	
1 tsp.	grated raw onion	

¾ tsp.	Worcestershire sauce
¼ tsp.	Tabasco
¼ tsp.	salt
2 Tblsp.	finely chopped walnuts
6 Tblsp.	finely chopped parsley

1. Drain salmon, discarding skin and bones.
2. Combine in a bowl the salmon, cream cheese, lemon juice, horseradish, onion, Worcestershire sauce, Tabasco, and salt. Beat until very smooth.
3. Turn into small, round bowl. Cover and refrigerate overnight.
4. Mix parsley and nuts on waxed paper. Roll salmon pâté in mixture to cover well.

Serve with crackers.

NICHOLAS KILBURN
Co-Principal Bassoon

. . . *Toronto possessed its first symphony orchestra in 1906 when the Toronto Conservatory Symphony Orchestra made its appearance under founder/conductor, Frank Welsman?*

. . . *such musical greats as Mischa Elman, Fritz Kreisler, and Sergei Rachmaninoff appeared with this orchestra?*

. . . *that on November 18, 1909, the weather was so cold that Sergei Rachmaninoff, who was appearing with the Toronto Conservatory Orchestra, had to rush to Messrs. Holt Renfrew to buy a fur cost?*

. . . *that in 1909 top orchestra seats went for $1.50 each with rush seats at 25 cents each?*

Serves 4 - 6   Borstch

1 lb.	spareribs	1 cup	shredded cabbage
6 cups	water	½ tsp.	pepper
6	beets, peeled and shredded	1 Tblsp.	salt
1	onion, diced	1 7½-oz.	can tomato sauce
1	carrot, diced		sour cream
1	large potato, diced		sprigs of fresh parsley

1. Boil spareribs for 1 hour in 6 cups water. Remove bones.
2. Add beets and cook for 45 minutes.
3. Add diced onion, carrot, potato, shredded cabbage, and seasonings. Cook for another half hour.
4. Add tomato sauce and cook for 15 minutes.

   Serve with sour cream on top and a sprig of parsley.

Long-time TS violinist Julian Kolkowski and his wife, Jennie, celebrate their Polish background with traditional, hearty recipes. Toronto-born Julian played with the Hart House Orchestra under Dr. Boyd Neel while a student at the University. He then joined The Toronto Symphony in the 1956-57 season.

JULIAN KOLKOWSKI
Principal, 2nd Violins

Serves 8

1 10-oz.	can tomato soup	1 package frozen okra (or canned)
1 10-oz.	can chicken gumbo	3 cups cooked seafood of your choice
1 10-oz.	can Manhattan clam chowder	(baby shrimps, crabmeat, scallops)
1 10-oz.	can chicken bouillon	¼ cup sherry
½ cup	chopped onion	2 cups hot cooked rice
2 Tblsp.	butter	

1. Combine soups and bouillon and heat almost to boiling.
2. Meanwhile, sauté chopped onion in butter; simmer frozen okra in water for 10 minutes; then slice.
3. Add cooked fish, onion, okra, and sherry to soup mixture, and heat to serving temperature.
4. When ready to serve, pack hot rice tightly into individual custard cups. Unmould one in the centre of each soup plate and pour hot gumbo around the rice.

Serve with salad and French bread.

The velvet voice of Maureen Forrester has been heard by audiences on five continents through her performances in opera, in concert, as soloist with virtually every major orchestra in the world, and on recordings. A former Montrealer, she studied with Bernard Diamant, making her Paris debut in 1955, followed soon after by a debut with the New York Philharmonic under Bruno Walter. In 1975 her debut with the Metropolitan Opera took place when she sang the role of Erda in Das Reingold. *A renowned Mahler exponent, Miss Forrester performed* Songs from "Des Knaben Wunderhorn" *when she accompanied the TS to Japan and China in 1978.*

MAUREEN FORRESTER
Contralto — Guest Artist

Serves 6

	conch meat (5 or more)	2	cobs corn
4-5 cups	water	2	large green peppers, chopped
1 Tblsp.	butter		tamari (very little)
2	large onions, chopped	1	bay leaf
2-5	garlic cloves, pressed		thyme (very little)
6-8	tomatoes, chopped (more if	pinch	Parmesan cheese
	chowder looks dry)		pepper (lots!)
2	large potatoes, chopped	3 or 4 pats	butter

1. Cut conch meat into small pieces and boil in just enough water to cover, adding more water if necessary. Cook until conch meat is tender, 3-5 hours.
2. Sauté onions and garlic in 1 Tblsp. butter until golden. Add tomatoes, potatoes, corn kernels, green pepper, tamari, bay leaf, thyme, Parmesan, and pepper. Cook over a very gentle heat for 5 minutes, stirring well. Remove from heat.
3. Add conch meat to vegetables when tender. Reduce conch liquid over a high heat by about one-quarter.
4. Add liquid to rest of ingredients.
5. Cook over a very low heat for 2-3 hours. Season with black pepper and a little butter.

This is a meal in itself, great with a salad. It is always better the next day when it is nice and ripe.

Note: Conch is a large shellfish very popular in the Caribbean region. It is unique tasting, but needs to cook for many hours. It can be purchased in good fish stores, particularly those catering to Caribbean people.

"I'm a rookie," says oboist Richard Dorsey cheerfully of his arrival on the Symphony scene for the 1979-80 season. Fresh from five years with the Stratford Ensemble, Richard is a Hartford, Connecticut native who studied music at Boston University and Catholic University in Washington, D.C. before coming to Canada. He picked up his Conch Chowder recipe before going to the Caribbean, he claims.

RICHARD DORSEY
Associate Principal Oboe

Serves 2

2 dozen	mussels, thoroughly scrubbed		½ tsp.	thyme
	olive oil to cover bottom of large		½ tsp.	oregano
	deep frying pan		½ tsp.	sage
3	cloves garlic, crushed		½ tsp.	marjoram
1	medium onion, chopped		¼ tsp.	pepper
3	large tomatoes, sliced		1 cup	dry white wine

1. Sauté garlic and onion in oil for 2 minutes.
2. Add tomatoes and seasonings. Cook for 2 more minutes.
3. Add wine and bring to the boil. Add mussels.
4. Cover and steam until mussels open (a few minutes only).
5. Discard any unopened mussels.

   Serve immediately in bowls garnished with parsley. Excellent with thick crusty Italian-type bread.

NORA SHULMAN
Associate Principal Flute

Serves 4 - 6

8	large carrots	1½ cups	strong chicken broth
2	onions	1 cup	table cream
½ cup	butter or margarine		sour cream for serving
3 Tblsp.	flour		grated carrot, dillweed or
1 tsp.	salt		nutmeg for serving

1. Cook carrots and onions in boiling salted water. Purée.
2. Melt butter, add flour and salt, and heat, stirring for 1 - 2 minutes.
3. Add broth slowly, stirring well.
4. Add purée. Heat to boiling, stirring until thick.
5. Cool slightly and add cream to desired consistency.

Serve, topping each bowl with sour cream, grated carrot, and a sprinkling of dillweed or nutmeg.

COROL McCARTNEY
Violin

Serves 4

1	large or 2 small potatoes		pepper
3	stalks celery	5 cups	water
1	carrot	1	onion, chopped
1	parsnip	2-3 Tblsp.	flour
	salt	2-3 Tblsp.	butter

1. Slice potatoes as for French fries; cut celery into small pieces; slice thinly or chop the carrot and parsnip.
2. Cook these vegetables in the 5 cups of water with salt and pepper to taste for 1 - 1½ hours.
3. Sauté the chopped onion in butter until soft but not browned. Sprinkle with flour and toss together. Add to the hot soup and simmer for a further half hour or more.

Esther Gartner loves the hearty vegetarian soup that her grandmother used to make in White Russia. It would be perfect for Saturday lunch at the ski chalet. Esther has little time for skiing, however. After graduating from the University of Toronto in 1970, she won a Canada Council grant to study in Lausanne for two years. She joined the TS in 1972 and during the last few years has performed in duets on CBC Radio. "Music, music, music — teaching and recitals — keeps me fulfilled," she says.

ESTHER GARTNER
Violoncello

Serves 6

4-6 Tblsp.	butter		1	package frozen green peas (2 cups)
½ lb.	mushrooms, thinly sliced		½	medium onion, finely chopped
2-3 Tblsp.	flour			salt and pepper
3 cups	chicken stock		2 cups	cream
½ tsp.	chervil			parsley

1. Melt 4 Tblsp. butter in a large pan and sauté mushrooms quickly for 2 minutes.
2. Remove mushrooms with slotted spoon and set them aside.
3. Add rest of butter and sprinkle with flour. Stir to blend.
4. Gradually add chicken stock and chervil, stirring constantly.
5. Cook, stirring, to boiling point. Soup will thicken slightly.
6. Add peas and onion and simmer for 10 minutes, stirring occasionally.
7. Blend soup, a little at a time in blender.
8. Return smooth purée to rinsed pan and add mushrooms, salt, and pepper.
9. Stir in cream and heat well.
10. Sprinkle chopped parsley on top.

NICHOLAS KILBURN
Co-Principal Bassoon

Serves 4 - 6

	dry mushrooms, a handful	½	onion, chopped
1 quart	water		salt, pepper, and paprika
1	small can chopped sauerkraut	¼ cup	flour
¼ cup	butter		

1. Soak dry mushrooms overnight. Rinse mushrooms well; then boil for 30 minutes and rinse again. Chop and boil them once more in 1 quart water, until they are tender.
2. Drain sauerkraut, reserving juice. Add sauerkraut to the mushrooms with enough reserved juice to make soup sour.
3. Melt butter and sauté onion until light brown. Add seasonings and add to soup.
4. Sauté flour in dry pan until light brown. Dilute with water or sauerkraut juice. Add to soup and bring to boil. Adjust seasonings if necessary.

Viola player Susan Lipchak brings together her background and that of her husband through her international cooking. Her Lemon Angel Dessert (p. 151) is as American as apple pie and once won her mother a $10 newspaper prize, while her husband's Slovakian ancestry is reflected in the recipe for Dry Mushroom Soup. In his family's Carpathian village the mushrooms would be smoked in the summer, then dried, and preserved for the winter. "It's hearty and delicious," says Susan, "great in cold weather. In Czechoslovakia it's traditionally served on Christmas Eve as one of several meatless dishes."

Chicago-born Susan is a graduate of DePauw University and the University of Michigan. From 1968 to 1970, she was Assistant Principal violist with the Toledo (Ohio) Symphony. She joined the TS in 1970.

SUSAN LIPCHAK
Assistant Principal Viola

Serves 4

1	package spinach	⅛ tsp.	nutmeg
2 cups	water	½ cup	half-and-half cream
2 Tblsp.	butter	1 Tblsp.	farina
3 Tblsp.	flour	4	hard-boiled eggs
1 10-oz.	can beef or chicken broth		croutons (optional)
½ tsp.	onion salt		juice of ½ - 1 lemon (optional)
¼ tsp.	white pepper		sour cream (optional)

1. Wash spinach well and cut off tough stems.
2. Place spinach in a saucepan. Add water, lightly salted, and boil spinach until tender.
3. Drain spinach, reserving water.
4. Melt butter in a saucepan.
5. Add flour and cook without browning.
6. When butter and flour begin to bubble, add spinach water.
7. Add beef or chicken broth. Bring to a boil.
8. Chop spinach.
9. Add spinach, onion salt, white pepper, nutmeg, cream, and farina to soup.
10. Boil for 5 - 6 minutes.
11. Before serving, add halved hard-boiled eggs and croutons. If desired, the juice of ½ - 1 lemon may be added. When serving, each bowl may be topped with a spoonful of sour cream.

STEPHANIE CHOMYK
Viola

Serves 8 - 10

Stock:

2-3 lb.	beef cut in cubes		4-6	carrots
¼ cup	vegetable oil		2-3	stalks celery
1	beef knuckle bone		2	onions, coarsely chopped
	salt and pepper to taste		1	handful parsley
2	cloves garlic		1 Tblsp.	horseradish
1 Tblsp.	thyme		1 Tblsp.	vinegar
2	bay leaves			

Soup:

4-5	carrots, sliced		1	package frozen peas, or equivalent fresh
2-3	potatoes, cubed		1	package frozen lima beans, or equivalent fresh
up to 1 lb.	fresh green beans, cut			
1	turnip, cubed		2	handfuls of alphabet or other soup noodles
1	package frozen corn, or equivalent amount of fresh		1	can tomato soup
1	large can tomatoes, preferably home-canned		½ - 1	can tomato paste, if desired

1. Brown beef. This is best done as follows: Put beef cubes in a mixing bowl with vegetable oil. Mix with hands so that all sides are covered with oil. Then brown. (Do not use any salt at this stage.)
2. When meat is browned, add remaining ingredients for stock, plus water to cover generously and then some. Bring to a gentle boil, reduce heat, and cook approximately 2 hours. Remove from heat. Refrigerate overnight. (This is your stock.)
3. The next day, or when ready to complete the soup, remove stock from the refrigerator and skim off fat. Remove vegetables from stock and either squeeze them over the stock to get their juices, or purée them in a blender or food processor and return them to the stock.
4. Reheat stock and add carrots, potatoes, green beans, and turnip.
5. About 20 minutes before above vegetables are done, add remaining ingredients.
6. Simmer all this gently as long as you like. It gets better with age.

Scott Wilson was born in Virginia, and it was there, in the Shenandoah Valley, that his family's vegetable soup recipe originated three or four generations ago. Scott began to play the French horn in high school in Washington, D.C., and studied at the Juilliard School of Music in New York before joining The Toronto Symphony in 1973. Besides his private teaching and freelancing, he is on the staff of the Faculty of Music, University of Toronto, and a member of the Toronto Chamber Winds and the Toronto Brass Society. He loves to cook and no kitchen chore is too much trouble for him.

SCOTT WILSON
Horn

Serves 4

2 lb.	pitted sour cherries		1 Tblsp.	cornstarch
1 cup	sugar		1 cup	red wine
3 cups	water		1 cup	35% cream
1	cinnamon stick		1-2 drops	almond extract

1. Simmer prepared cherries with sugar, water, and cinnamon until tender.
2. Mix cornstarch with a little water to make a smooth paste. Add a little hot liquid and return thickening to pan.
3. Bring to a boil and remove from heat. Remove cinnamon stick.
4. Cool; stir in wine, cream, and almond extract.

Serve well chilled in a large glass bowl. It is sinfully good!

"I do all the cooking at our house," says Symphony member Daniel Ruddick. "I collect cookbooks, and my ideal vacation is going to New York or San Francisco for the great restaurants." His Cold Cherry Soup is an old Hungarian recipe.

Daniel was born outside Cleveland, studied there and at Ohio State University, and played with various small orchestras for ten years before coming to Toronto in 1971. He joined The Toronto Symphony in 1973.

DANIEL RUDDICK
Percussion

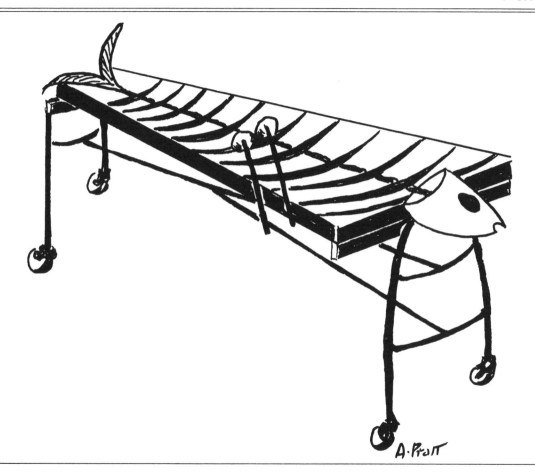

A. Pratt

Serves 6 - 8

1	large red snapper (minimum 3 lb.)	1½ cups	olive oil
	salt and pepper	pinch	finely chopped parsley
	a few slices of lemon and onion	3 oz.	ground almonds
2	yolks of hard-boiled eggs		seedless wedges of 3 oranges
2	raw egg yolks		
	juice of 1 lime		

1. Clean fish and remove head. Place head and fish in a pot and cover with water. Add salt and pepper to taste and a few slices of lemon and onion.
2. Cook over very low heat until cooked but still firm.
3. Set head aside. Remove skin and bones from fish. Place red snapper on serving dish and refrigerate 2 - 3 hours or overnight.
4. Place boiled and raw egg yolks in blender and add the lime juice a few drops at a time. While mixing at medium speed, add olive oil slowly until you obtain a firm mayonnaise.
5. Combine parsley, almonds, and salt, and add this mixture gradually to the mayonnaise. Refrigerate.

   Serve fish cold with head in place. Cover the fish with mayonnaise and decorate with wedges of orange.

Eduardo Mata is a native of Mexico, where he is highly esteemed for his contribution to the music of his country. A popular guest conductor, he has made appearances with orchestras all over the world. In 1977, he was appointed Music Director of the Dallas Symphony Orchestra, and in 1978, he accepted a permanent association with the London Symphony Orchestra.

EDUARDO MATA
Guest Conductor

Serves 6

    1 3-lb.   flounder
    1 cup   dry white wine

Deviled Crab Stuffing:

2 cups	fresh or frozen crabmeat	¼ tsp.	salt
1 Tblsp.	butter	1½ tsp.	Dijon mustard
1½ Tblsp.	cracker crumbs	1	healthy pinch cayenne
¾ cup	whipping cream		a few capers, if desired
1	egg		

1. At the fish market have the fishmonger (1) remove the head and tail of the flounder, clean and scale it, (2) open the fish "like a book", i.e., slit the fish open on one side and separate meat from bones on both sides of the spine, stopping just short of the side you wish to leave intact. The fish will then fall open leaving the spine and ribs in the middle, which can then be cut off as near as possible to the intact side. Now you're ready to stuff it.
2. To make stuffing, flake crabmeat. Set aside.
3. Melt butter in saucepan, add crumbs and cream, and cook until thick, stirring constantly.
4. Remove from heat, add remaining ingredients, and mix well.
5. Add crabmeat.
6. Set oven to 375° F.
7. Stuff the flounder with deviled crab mixture. Then sew the fish tightly closed with needle and strong thread. Use a thimble as the skin of raw flounder is tough.
8. Place the fish in buttered baking dish and pour white wine over it. Dot with butter or drape with 1 or 2 strips of bacon. Cook uncovered, basting every so often with wine and pan juices until fish is done, approximately 30 minutes.

SCOTT WILSON
Horn

Serves 4

1½ lb.	white fish (cod, haddock, etc.)		pinch	cayenne pepper (or to taste)
1	medium onion		¼ cup	creamed coconut (available at
1 Tblsp.	laos powder (available at Dutch			West Indian grocery stores)
	grocery stores)			juice of ½ lemon
1 tsp.	paprika		1 cup	water
1 tsp.	turmeric			

1. Chop the onion finely and sauté in oil until soft.
2. Add spices and cook a few minutes longer.
3. Add creamed coconut and stir until melted.
4. Add lemon juice and water. Stir until mixed.
5. Add fish and simmer for 5 minutes. Serve immediately.

Peter Madgett, double bass with the TS since 1978 and husband of soprano Mary Lou Fallis, has contributed an Indonesian recipe arising from his love of Indian cooking. "I've just expanded and moved eastward," he explains. "Much as I love Indian cooking, I find Indonesian a little more delicate. It doesn't have the body, the full taste."

Toronto-born, Peter studied at the University of Toronto under TS principal bass Tom Monohan. He played with the Chamber Players of Toronto for four years and was Principal Bass of the Hamilton Philharmonic for three years before joining the Symphony.

PETER MADGETT
Double Bass

Serves 6

24	mussels or clams		6 Tblsp.	dill weed, chopped
1 lb.	shrimp		1	clove garlic, minced
1½ cups	mayonnaise (Make your own; it will taste better.)		1 Tblsp.	lemon juice

1. Thoroughly wash mussels. Beards may be discarded or left, as you please. Throw out any open mussels.
2. Steam in own juice until open, for about 7 minutes. Throw out any that do not open.
3. Boil and shell shrimp.
4. Arrange mussels on half shell on a platter. Retain mussel juice. Place shrimp on platter.
5. Prepare mayonnaise; add dill, garlic, and lemon juice. Allow to sit for 3 hours. If too thick, add mussel juice.
6. Spoon sauce over mussels and serve at room temperature.

NORA SHULMAN
Associate Principal Flute

Serves 3 - 4   A Food Processor Recipe

1 lb.	fresh or thawed sole (or haddock)	lemon slices and extra corn
¼	green pepper	flake crumbs
1 cup	grated Cheddar cheese	
¼ cup	corn flake crumbs	
1	small cooking onion	optional seasoning:
1½ oz.	sherry (or to taste)	2 Tblsp. chopped fresh parsley
	salt and pepper	1 Tblsp. chopped fresh dill

1. Set oven to 350° F.
2. Using metal blade, place chunks of green pepper in food processor bowl. Process until finely chopped.
3. Add fish cut in chunks and process for a few seconds.
4. Add remaining ingredients (except lemon slices) and process very lightly until just mixed.
5. Place individual portions into small buttered oven proof dishes.
6. Sprinkle more corn flake crumbs on top and add a slice of lemon.
7. Bake 20 minutes.

VARIATIONS: Stir in bits of shrimp, scallop, or lobster before spooning mixture into prepared dishes.

"I like to cook and entertain," says TS member Richard Cohen. "I thumb through my wife's cookbooks, read the ingredients, and improvise from there." Brooklyn-born Richard recalls his first cooking experience: "It was on my first trip to Canada, at the age of 15, on a bicycling tour through the Rockies. I was the only one who had an inkling of cooking so I found myself feeding nine people." He devised the preceding recipe to tempt his young children to eat fish. The addition of corn flakes worked, he says, because "they like crunchy things".

A graduate of the Eastman School of Music and the Cleveland Institute of Music, Richard joined The Toronto Symphony as a horn player in 1972.

RICHARD COHEN
Horn

Serves 4 - 6

	pastry for 9-inch pie shell		½ cup	milk
1 cup	Swiss cheese, grated		½ cup	mayonnaise
2	eggs		2 Tblsp.	flour
⅓ cup	chopped scallions		1 7¾-oz.	can salmon

1. Set oven to 425° F.
2. Prepare pastry and line pie plate. Don't prick. Cover bottom of pastry with a piece of foil to keep it from bubbling during baking.
3. Place on bottom rack of oven and bake for 10 minutes.
4. Remove, and reduce oven to 350° F.
5. Remove skin and bones from salmon, and flake.
6. Beat eggs, add scallions, milk, mayonnaise, flour, and beat again. Add flaked salmon.
7. Cover bottom of pastry with grated cheese.
8. Pour salmon mixture into prepared base.
9. Bake 45 minutes or until a knife inserted in the centre comes out clean.

VERA TARNOWSKY
Violin

Serves 4

1 7¾-oz.	can salmon		dash	cayenne
	milk		½ tsp.	dry mustard
3 Tblsp.	butter		4	eggs, separated
3 Tblsp.	flour		1 tsp.	Worcestershire sauce
¼ tsp.	salt			paprika

1. Set oven to 350° F.
2. Drain salmon liquid into 8-oz. measuring cup and add enough milk to make 1 cup. Flake salmon.
3. In pan melt butter. Blend in flour, salt, cayenne, and mustard.
4. Gradually add milk and cook until thick and smooth.
5. Remove from heat and stir in beaten yolks, Worcestershire sauce, and salmon. Cool.
6. Beat egg whites until stiff but not dry, and fold gently into mixture.
7. Pour into buttered 2-quart soufflé dish and bake 45-50 minutes.
8. Sprinkle with paprika and serve with salad of your choice.

Stephanie Chomyk's Ukrainian mother was one of those old-fashioned cooks who worked magic in the kitchen without measuring anything. Cooking is a joy to Stephanie and she loves adapting her mother's recipes to Canadian measurements. "I enjoy the challenge of experimenting with old family dishes," she says.

A graduate in viola of the Royal Conservatory of Music in Toronto, Stephanie also gets a thrill out of playing different instruments such as the mandolin, guitar, and harp. Her longtime dedication to the TS began in 1953.

STEPHANIE CHOMYK
Viola

Serves 4

¼ cup	butter or margarine	2 cups	cereal (light) cream
1	green pepper, seeded and cut into thin strips	7½ oz.	crabmeat (can is simplest) drained, boned, flaked, juice reserved
1	red pepper, seeded and cut into thin strips	2 Tblsp.	melted butter or margarine
1 lb.	mushrooms, sliced	3 Tblsp.	flour (or more)
1 Tblsp.	lemon juice	¼ cup	grated Swiss Emmenthaler or Parmesan cheese
½ tsp.	salt, or to taste		

1. Melt butter or margarine in large skillet over medium heat. Add green and red peppers; cook until tender. Add mushrooms and sprinkle with lemon juice and salt. Cook 2 minutes, tossing occasionally.
2. Add cream and reserved crabmeat liquid. Bring to boil.
3. In a small saucepan over low heat, combine melted butter or margarine and flour; blend until smooth. Stir flour mixture into creamed vegetable mixture.
4. Cook, stirring constantly, until sauce has thickened and is smooth.
5. Add crabmeat. Simmer 1 to 2 minutes or until crabmeat is heated through. Season to taste.
6. Divide mixture among 6 shells or ramekins, or turn into a 1-quart shallow baking dish.
7. Sprinkle with cheese. Place under broiler until cheese is golden brown.

If using shells or ramekins, place them on a cookie sheet; otherwise you'll have a giant mess! This is good as an appetizer or as a main dish, served with steamed rice and a spring herb salad.

TS tuba player Hubert Meyer doubles in brass as the Orchestra's personnel manager. In his spare time he displays further artistry in carpentry and woodwork. His equally busy wife, Ina, works as his secretary and Girl Friday — and does the cooking.

HUBERT MEYER
Tuba

. . . *that Toronto's first Symphony orchestra couldn't survive World War I? Music lovers were buying Victory Bonds instead of tickets.*

. . . *Toronto's second symphony orchestra started when two pupils of Viennese conductor/teacher Luigi von Kunits persuaded him to form the New Symphony Orchestra in 1922 and that it was manned by professional musicians who earned their livings in vaudeville and movie theatres such as Shea's and the Uptown?*

. . . *that these musicians played in the orchestra for sheer love of classical music and a share in the profits — usually $4.00 per concert?*

Serves 2 - 4

1 2-3 lb.	frying chicken	
½ cup	yogurt	
½ cup	lime juice	
½ cup	white wine	

paprika or chili powder
2 lemons or limes, chopped
1 handful of chopped parsley

1. Set oven to 325° F.
2. Skin chicken and discard skin.
3. Dip chicken in mixture of yogurt, lime juice, and white wine to coat completely.
4. Sprinkle with paprika or chili powder.
5. Inside cavity put chopped lemons and/or limes and parsley.
6. Reduce oven temperature to 225° F. and roast chicken slowly for 45 minutes. Turn off oven heat, but leave chicken in oven until cool. Do not open oven door after turning off heat.
7. Chill in refrigerator. Discard stuffing.

Serve cold with a green salad and a well chilled dry white wine.

Tom Monohan is famous for his cooking. Born in the United States, he earned a degree from the Curtis Institute. In 1966 he joined The Toronto Symphony, and is now a Canadian citizen. In addition to his Symphony performances, Tom has been involved in every aspect of music in Toronto — education, studio, film, and chamber groups. He teaches at the University of Toronto, the Royal Conservatory of Music, and the Banff School of Fine Arts, and he coaches the National Youth Orchestra and the Toronto Symphony Youth Orchestra. Although music makes up a large part of his life, he loves fine cuisine and is willing to make time for its creation.

THOMAS MONOHAN
Principal Double Bass

Serves 4

	cooking oil		2 Tblsp.	lemon juice
2-3 lb.	chicken, cut up		1 Tblsp.	Worcestershire sauce
	salt, pepper, poultry seasoning		1 Tblsp.	vinegar
¼ cup	diced onion		1 Tblsp.	mustard
¼ cup	diced green pepper		1 Tblsp.	molasses
¼ cup	diced celery		1 Tblsp.	water (if needed)
¼ - ⅓ cup	bottled barbecue sauce		½ tsp.	chili powder
¼ cup	catsup		dash	sage and oregano

1. Set oven to 350° F.
2. Season chicken with salt and pepper and/or poultry seasoning and fry in a small amount of oil until chicken is almost cooked (about 20 minutes). Remove.
3. Sauté onion, green pepper, and celery in oil until tender. Remove.
4. In an oil-free pan place remaining ingredients with onion, peppers, and celery. Cook over medium heat for 10 to 15 minutes.
5. Place chicken pieces in a single layer and cover with sauce. Cover and bake for about 30 minutes.

Percussionist Donald Kuehn made the trek from hometown Denver to Toronto and the TS in 1973 via Boston University and a stint as assistant timpanist with the Baltimore Symphony. Don has frequently been featured on children's T.V. shows and plays in the Symphony's education programs in schools, libraries, and hospitals. An ardent cook, he shares kitchen time with wife, Beth.

DONALD KUEHN
Principal Percussion

Serves 4

4	large chicken breasts, halved		1 tsp.	salt
1 6-oz.	can frozen orange juice, thawed		½ tsp.	ginger
⅓ cup	honey		¼ tsp.	nutmeg
1 tsp.	paprika		pinch	pepper

1. Set oven to 350° F.
2. Grease a baking dish that is just large enough for the chicken.
3. Arrange chicken in pan, skin side down.
4. Combine all remaining ingredients and pour over chicken.
5. Bake for 30 minutes; turn chicken over and continue to bake for another 30 minutes, basting frequently.
6. Remove from oven; continue to baste with remaining sauce as chicken cools.

   Serve cold.

Violist Marilyn Meyer's festive but "quick and easy" baked chicken is a constant winner at orchestra parties. She says a dash of cognac or Grand Marnier adds that gala feeling.

Chicago-born, Marilyn studied at Philadelphia's Curtis Institute of Music, joined The Toronto Symphony in 1960, and currently runs an antiques business in addition to her musical life.

MARILYN J. MEYER
Viola

Serves 8

12	chicken pieces (breasts and legs)
1½ tsp.	marjoram
2 10-oz.	cans mushroom soup
10 oz.	milk
¼ tsp.	mace

4 Tblsp.	butter
½ cup	sliced blanched almonds
2 cups	coarse soft bread crumbs
½ cup	sherry

1. Set oven to 350° F.
2. Arrange chicken pieces in a flat pan which has been greased with bacon fat.
3. Sprinkle heavily with marjoram.
4. Cover with mixture of soup, milk, and mace.
5. Bake for 30 minutes.
6. Fry the almonds in butter until lightly browned.
7. Mix in bread crumbs and sprinkle over the chicken.
8. Drizzle with sherry and bake 30 minutes longer.

Ezra Schabas, Principal of the Royal Conservatory of Music in Toronto, has been involved in Canadian music since the early fifties, when he came from New York to teach at the Conservatory and to work in its Concert Bureau and Public Relations Department. After eight years as Chairman of the Performance Department in the Faculty of Music, University of Toronto, he became Principal of the Conservatory in 1978.

Principal Schabas has been the moving force behind the new Orchestral Training Programme which provides young professional musicians with orchestral experience under different guest conductors.

For relaxation, Juilliard-trained Ezra Schabas likes to play his clarinet.

EZRA SCHABAS
Principal, Royal Conservatory of Music

Serves 16 - 20   (for chicken-hating bassoonists)

    4   large chickens, cut up

Sauce:

1 cup	medium dry white wine		4 Tblsp.	honey
½ cup	vegetable oil		4 Tblsp.	soya sauce
½ cup	ketchup		4 Tblsp.	beef bouillon
	juice of 2 lemons		1 tsp.	oregano leaves
4 Tblsp.	vinegar		1½ tsp.	ground ginger
2 Tblsp.	brown sugar		1¼ tsp.	marjoram leaves
2 Tblsp.	paprika		1 tsp.	pepper
2 Tblsp.	onion powder		dash	cayenne pepper
4 Tblsp.	molasses		3	cloves garlic, minced

1. Set oven to 400° F.
2. Mix together all ingredients for sauce and simmer until heated through.
3. Place chicken pieces in a large flat roasting pan.
4. Pour sauce over chicken, cover and bake for 30 minutes at 400° F. Uncover and bake for 45 minutes longer at 350° F., basting frequently.

This dish is good cold if there is any left over, and the sauce is great with meat balls or as a marinade for steak.

CHRISTOPHER WEAIT
Co-Principal Bassoon

Serves 6

3	chicken breasts, split and boned (6 pieces)		6 tsp.	currants
6	thin slices lean ham		1 cup	chicken broth mixed with
6	dried apricots, sliced		1 Tblsp.	dry vermouth
6	water chestnuts, sliced		½ cup	sliced almonds

1. Set oven to 350° F.
2. Pound chicken breasts until flat and thin.
3. Cover each breast with a slice of ham, 1 apricot, 1 water chestnut, 1 tsp. currants.
4. Roll up breast and secure with a toothpick.
5. Place in a shallow, greased baking dish.
6. Cover with broth.
7. Sprinkle with almond slices.
8. Bake 45 minutes, covered.
9. Uncover and bake a further 15 minutes to brown.

COROL McCARTNEY
Violin

Serves 4

1	frying chicken		1	small tomato, chopped
1	large onion, diced			salt
	corn oil		½-1 cup	water
2 tsp.	Hungarian sweet red paprika		1 tsp.	flour
½	medium green pepper, cut up		½ cup	sour cream

1. Cut up chicken, separating leg and thigh and cutting breast into four pieces.
2. Cook onion in a little oil until light golden brown.
3. Remove pan from heat and add enough paprika to make a good red colour. Be careful *not* to burn the paprika.
4. Add chicken, green pepper, tomato, salt to taste, and water. Stir thoroughly. The juice should nearly cover the chicken.
5. Cover and simmer, stirring occasionally with a wooden spoon for approximately 1 - 1½ hours, until chicken is tender.
6. When chicken is cooked, make a smooth paste with 1 tsp. flour and a little water. Add to sour cream. Add mixture to chicken. Bring just to a boil; then serve with Hungarian dumplings.

DUMPLINGS

3 eggs	salt
3 cups all-purpose flour	water

1. Beat eggs with a little salt.
2. Add flour and enough water (approximately ½ - 1 cup) to make dough the consistency of bread dough.
3. Have ready a large pan of boiling salted water.
4. Cut strips off the mound of dough and then cut into fingertip-size pieces; roll lightly into balls.
5. Drop pieces into boiling water, one by one, and stir gently so that dumplings do not stick to the bottom of pan.
6. Dumplings are done when they rise to the top, about 10 minutes.

Serve with Chicken Paprikas, pouring a little sauce on top.

George Horvath shares some treasured Hungarian recipes with us in this book. He says, "For a traditional Hungarian dinner, serve Chicken Paprikas with Hungarian Dumplings, Sour Cream Cucumber Salad (p.107), and Chestnut Sponge Cake (p. 129)".

George has been a member of The Toronto Symphony since 1952 and is one of the many Symphony musicians who bring their love of music to Toronto school children. In addition to teaching, he is in demand for solo recitals and various chamber music ensembles.

GEORGE HORVATH
Violoncello

Serves 8

Filling:

½ cup	chopped onion
¼ cup	chopped celery
¼ cup	butter
¾ cup	sliced mushrooms
1 tsp.	lemon juice
2 cups	cooked diced chicken
¼ cup	condensed cream of mushroom soup
½	clove garlic, minced
¼ tsp.	black pepper
	salt to taste

Dough:

2 cups	biscuit mix
½ cup	milk

Sauce:

1½ cups	sliced mushrooms
2 tsp.	butter
½ cup	condensed cream of mushroom soup
2 tsp.	chopped parsley
2 tsp.	lemon juice

1. To make the filling, sauté onion and celery in butter until golden.
2. Add mushrooms and lemon juice. Sauté 2 minutes longer.
3. Add chicken, soup, garlic, salt, and pepper. Stir.
4. Remove from heat, cover and chill for 30 minutes.
5. Set oven to 400° F.
6. To make the dough, lightly combine the milk and biscuit mix. Knead on lightly floured board. Roll into rectangle 18 x 7 inches.
7. Spread filling evenly down centre of dough. Moisten one long edge and roll up jelly-roll style, toward moistened edge. Press seams to seal. Moisten both ends. Shape roll into a ring, pinching ends together to seal. Cut slits in ring.

8. Brush with 1 egg beaten with 1 tsp. water. Slide onto greased baking sheet and bake 20 - 25 minutes.
9. To make the sauce, sauté mushrooms in butter.
10. Add soup, parsley, and lemon juice. Stir constantly.
11. Serve hot over chicken ring.

John Gowen prefers baseball to cooking, but he has submitted his wife's recipes for two of his favourite dishes.

John's interest in the double bass began with his school orchestra in Toronto. Teaching now takes up much of his spare time, but he is still an ardent baseball player with The Toronto Symphony baseball team.

JOHN GOWEN
Double Bass

Serves 4

2	whole chicken breasts, skinned, boned and cut into bite-size pieces	1	can condensed cream of chicken soup
	pepper	½ cup	mayonnaise
1 Tblsp.	oil	2 Tblsp.	lemon juice
2	cans of asparagus tips or cuttings, fresh or frozen	1 tsp.	curry powder
		1 cup	shredded sharp Cheddar cheese

1. Set oven to 375° F.
2. Grease 9 x 9 x 2-inch baking dish.
3. Sprinkle chicken with freshly ground pepper. Sauté slowly in oil until lightly browned. Remove from heat and drain well.
4. Cut asparagus, if using whole tips, into 1-inch pieces. Spread in bottom of dish.
5. Place chicken over asparagus.
6. In a bowl mix together soup, mayonnaise, lemon juice, and curry powder. Pour over chicken and asparagus. Sprinkle with cheese.
7. Bake for about 30 minutes.

In her busy career with The Toronto Symphony, Georgina Roberts has still found time to make her family's favourite dishes and her own clothes.

While at the Royal Conservatory of Music, Georgina studied both piano and cello. Her cello teacher was Marcus Adeney, for many years a distinguished TS cellist. He encouraged her to join the orchestra in 1951, under Sir Ernest MacMillan, in the double role of keyboard player and cellist. Now she plays only the cello in the orchestra, but continues to play the piano for her own pleasure.

GEORGINA ROBERTS
Violoncello

Serves 6 - 8

1 6-8 lb.	goose	**Sauce:**	
3 Tblsp.	vegetable oil	¾ cup	18% cream
1 lb.	onions, sliced	½ lb.	button mushrooms, halved
8	cloves garlic, chopped	1 lb.	small onions
2 Tblsp.	chopped parsley	3 Tblsp.	butter
6	tomatoes, chopped	1 Tblsp.	sugar
	salt and pepper		
2 cups	apple juice		

1. Set oven to 325° F.
2. Wipe goose and dry. Prick with fork all over. Brown in vegetable oil in roasting pan.
3. Remove goose from roasting pan and set aside. To pan add onions, garlic, parsley, tomatoes, salt and pepper to taste. Cook 5 minutes.
4. Replace goose on top of vegetables and pour apple juice over it. Cover and bake for 3 hours, basting twice.
5. Remove goose to heated serving platter and keep warm.
6. To make sauce, skim fat from roasting pan and add cream. Then add mushrooms which have been sautéed in 1 Tblsp. oil for 5 minutes.
7. Add onions which have been glazed in butter and sugar.
8. Pour sauce over goose or disjoint into small pieces and cover with sauce.

COROL McCARTNEY
Violin

Serves 2

2 1-1½ lb.   hens

Stuffing:

2 Tblsp.	butter		⅛ tsp.	salt
2 Tblsp.	sliced green onions, including tops		dash	pepper
½ cup	toasted slivered almonds		½ cup	cooked long grain rice
4 Tblsp.	snipped parsley			

Burgundy Glaze:

½ cup	red burgundy		2 tsp.	cornstarch
2 Tblsp.	butter		2 tsp.	Worcestershire sauce
2 Tblsp.	lemon juice		½ tsp.	allspice
½ cup	black currant jelly		dash	salt and pepper

1. Set oven to 400° F.
2. Melt butter and sauté onions until tender.
3. Remove from heat and stir in the almonds, parsley, salt, and pepper.
4. Add the cooked rice and toss lightly to mix.
5. Salt, stuff, and truss the hens.

6. Cook in a shallow pan for about 1½ hours, covering loosely with foil for the first 30 minutes. Uncover and baste frequently with the burgundy glaze for the remaining hour of cooking.
7. To make the burgundy glaze, combine all the ingredients in a saucepan and cook until the mixture thickens and boils, stirring constantly. Remove from heat and use to glaze birds during cooking. The remaining glaze should be used as a sauce when serving.

This recipe may be easily adjusted to suit individual needs. I like to serve it with broccoli in lemon butter sauce: melt 4 oz. (½ cup) butter and add 1 oz. (2 Tblsp.) lemon juice.

Oboist Frank Morphy is an ardent cook — when he isn't pitching for the TS baseball team or bartending at the Symphony Rummage Sale, that is.

Born in Ottawa, Frank began his musical career by playing the trombone in his high school band. He moved on to the oboe, the National Youth Orchestra, and study at the University of Toronto. This was followed by three years with the National Ballet orchestra and summer teaching at the Banff School of Fine Arts. His dreams were realized when he became a member of The Toronto Symphony in 1973.

FRANK MORPHY
Oboe

Serves 6

1	hare or large wild rabbit, jointed

Marinade:

	a little oil		seasoned flour
1	medium carrot, sliced		a little lard
1	large or 2 small onions, chopped	½ lb.	bacon
1 or 2	sticks of celery, diced	1	large onion
1	clove garlic		chopped parsley
1	sprig of parsley, chopped		thyme, a large pinch
pinch	thyme	1-2 cups	beef stock
1	bay leaf	3 oz.	port
8	peppercorns	1 Tblsp.	coarse-cut marmalade
6	coriander seeds (optional)		salt, pepper
6	juniper berries (essential)		a little lemon juice
1	bottle of red wine		

1. First shoot your hare! (The creature should be 'hung' for a few days; like all game it should be 'high'.) Keep the brains, blood, and liver to thicken the sauce at the end.
2. Place the jointed hare in a bowl or casserole.
3. Prepare the marinade as follows:
   In a saucepan, brown the carrot, onion, celery, and garlic lightly in a little oil. Stir in the herbs and spices and cook gently for 2 or 3 minutes; then add the wine. Bring to a boil and simmer gently for 30 minutes.
4. Let the marinade get completely cold before you pour it onto the pieces of hare; the meat should be marinated for at least 8 hours and can be left for up to 2 days.

After this lengthy Adagio introduction, we come at last to the Allegro . . .

5. Set oven to 300° F.
6. Take the pieces of hare from the marinade; let them drain thoroughly, and dip them in the seasoned flour.
7. Fry the bacon and onions in lard (you won't need much if the bacon is fatty).
8. Add the meat and brown it, and transfer the lot to a casserole.
9. Throw in the herbs and, using 1 part marinade to 2 parts beef stock, add just enough liquid to cover.
10. Now cover the casserole and put in oven for about 3 hours. The meat should be tender and part easily from the bone.
11. Add the port, marmalade, and seasoning to taste.

Now comes the thickening process . . .

12. Mash the blood, brains, and liver together. Pour in a little of the hot liquid and return this mixture to the pot. Cook this gently for a few minutes until it thickens. On *no* account must you allow it to boil at this stage. The blood, like eggs, will curdle. Alternatively, for those of you with weak stomachs (but this is a poor alternative), you may simply thicken the sauce with little knobs of flour and butter.
13. Immediately before serving, sharpen with a little lemon juice.

The best accompaniments to this princely dish are red cabbage and dumplings.

DUMPLINGS

4 oz.	flour (1 cup)	1 Tblsp.	chopped parsley and olives (or other herbs, according to your whim)
1 tsp.	baking powder		water
1	healthy pinch of salt		creamed or grated horseradish
2 oz.	shredded suet		beef stock

1. Sieve together the flour, baking powder, and salt.
2. Mix in the suet and herbs, and add just enough water to make a very slightly sticky dough.
3. Cover your hands with flour and roll the dough into little balls. These will swell as they cook.
4. Poke a little horseradish into the centre of each dumpling and poach them gently in the beef stock for 10 - 20 minutes. When they are done, you can dump them (ouch!) in with the hare.

One of the stars of the world's new generation of conductors, English-born Andrew Davis, Music Director of The Toronto Symphony, has continued to expand his international reputation since taking over the TS baton in 1975. In the last few years guest conducting with major orchestras has led him to Chicago, New York, Cleveland, Philadelphia, Boston, Los Angeles, Milan, Rome, Paris, and London. He has made his debut with both the Berlin Philharmonic Orchestra and the Stockholm Philharmonic. His appearances with major festivals include Edinburgh, Flanders, and Berlin, and he has conducted at the Glyndebourne Opera Festival for several summers.

ANDREW DAVIS
Music Director

A. Pratt

Serves 6 - 8

3-4 lb.	rump roast	2-3	large bay leaves
¾ cup	red wine vinegar	1 tsp.	mustard
¾ cup	red wine	1 tsp.	salt
½ cup	bouillon broth (from cubes or can)	2½-3 Tblsp.	flour
1 cup	water		milk or sour cream
1 Tblsp.	chopped dried onions		

1. Combine vinegar, red wine, bouillon broth, and water. Add onions, bay leaves, mustard, and salt. Stir and heat slightly; then let mixture cool.
2. Put roast in a plastic bag in a crock. Pour mixture over roast, making sure at least half of the meat is covered in crock, and marinate for 2 - 3 days in refrigerator, turning meat over twice a day.
3. Remove roast from marinade and pat it dry.
4. Brown meat on all sides in a small amount of fat in strong cooking pot.
5. Pour marinade over roast. Simmer for 2 - 2½ hours, until meat is tender.
6. Remove meat and keep it warm. Strain marinade. Mix flour with water, stirring it into a thick paste. Then add marinade, stir and cook, thinning it down with milk or sour cream. Other seasonings such as soy sauce and sugar can be added to taste.

Encouraged by his German-born musician parents, James Wallenberg began violin lessons at the age of nine at school in Binghamton, New York. Later, he moved on to Ithaca College where he received a degree in music education in 1974. This was followed by three years at the Yale Graduate School of Music. He then freelanced in Boston for a year before joining the TS in 1978.

James says this recipe is his mother's, and it is "really excellent".

JAMES WALLENBERG
Violin

Serves 2

Solomon Sukiyaki

2 Tblsp.	peanut oil
2	large onions, chopped
2	large stalks celery, chopped
1	whole green pepper, chopped
½ dozen	or more large mushrooms

1	sirloin steak, approximately
	¼ inch thick
	rice or noodles
	dried noodles or almond slices
	soya sauce

1. Heat oil in cast-iron pan.
2. Add onions and stir.
3. Add celery and stir.
4. Add green pepper and stir.
5. Slice mushrooms thickly and add.
6. Cut off fat from steak and slice steak into small pieces about ⅛ inch thick.
7. Add meat to vegetables; turn heat up to brown meat for a few minutes; then turn off element.
8. Cook rice or noodles and place on large platter. Pour meat and vegetables over rice or noodles. Sprinkle with dried noodles or almonds and a dash of soya sauce.

"Schiderein a bissel zalts" ("throw in a little salt") or "a bissel something else" was Stanley Solomon's Jewish grandmother's way of concocting wonderful dishes. Stanley's own weekday cooking — his wife cooks on weekends — has the same air of improvised zest. Calling himself a short-order cook rather than a gourmet one, he stirs up a storm with crisp green vegetables and steak.

Stanley's career as violist with The Toronto Symphony spans more than thirty years during which he found time to play with the Kathleen Parlow Quartet and to act as violist/manager with the Hart House Orchestra.

STANLEY SOLOMON
Principal Viola

Serves 5 - 6   Meat-filled Dough

Dough:

3	eggs
½ tsp.	salt
pinch	pepper
2½ cups	all-purpose flour

Filling:

1 lb.	beef chuck in chunks
2	large onions, sliced
2 Tblsp.	chicken fat or margarine
1	egg
	salt and pepper to taste
3 quarts	boiling salted water

1. In a bowl beat eggs, salt, and pepper. Add flour to make a soft dough.
2. Put dough on a floured board. Knead 5 minutes until smooth. Roll out very thinly. If too thick, the finished product will be too doughy.
3. Do not allow dough to dry. Shape into 2-inch squares with a knife.
4. To make the filling, fry meat and onions in fat. Add egg, salt, and pepper, and mix well.
5. Place 1 tsp. of meat on each square of dough. Fold over in triangle. Pressure seal edges.
6. Boil triangles in boiling, salted water for 20 minutes.

Russian-born Jascha Milkis has chosen a recipe from his homeland. This version of ravioli originated in Siberia where the resourceful inhabitants would make and freeze hundreds of them to eat during the long winter. Now a popular dish all over Russia, Pelmeni can be heated in soup, or eaten with sour cream.

Jascha Milkis's violin studies in Odessa and Moscow were followed by a career as soloist, and as concertmaster with the Odessa Symphony Orchestra and the Leningrad Opera and Theatre Orchestra. Then, after twenty years with the Leningrad Symphony Orchestra, he came to Canada and joined the TS in 1975.

JASCHA MILKIS
Associate Concertmaster

Serves 6 - 8

2 lb.	round steak, cut into 1-inch cubes	1	can sliced mushrooms or 1 lb. fresh mushrooms
1 1½-oz.	package onion soup mix	1 cup	dry red wine (or more)

1. Set oven to 325° F.
2. Sauté beef cubes quickly in a little oil.
3. Place beef and onion soup mix in large casserole with mushrooms and liquid, and add wine.
4. Cover and bake for 2 hours, stirring occasionally.
5. Cool and freeze if desired. When re-heating, add 1 can mushroom soup.

Serve with rice or garlic bread and salad.

Symphony oboist Stanley Wood unwinds from concert tension with his oil painting. Some of his happiest moments are spent on country painting expeditions when he and wife Betty picnic on Scotch Eggs while the Beef Bourguignon simmers slowly at home.

A TS member since 1956, Oshawa-born Stanley studied in Canada and the United States and was a founding member of the Winnipeg Symphony in 1947.

STANLEY WOOD
Oboe

Serves 4 - 6

5-6	small eggs		1 tsp.	salt
1 lb.	sausage meat			freshly ground pepper
1 tsp.	dried sage or 1 tsp. poultry seasoning		½ cup	dried bread crumbs, lightly seasoned

1. Set oven to 325° F.
2. Hard boil eggs; cool in cold water.
3. Mix sausage meat, sage or poultry seasoning, salt, and pepper.
4. Mould 2 tsp. (approximately) sausage mixture around each chilled, shelled egg.
5. Roll in the bread crumbs, covering completely and shaping neatly.
6. Bake 30 - 40 minutes, turning often. If the meat starts to separate, lower heat.

These are delicious served hot or cold and are ideal for a picnic or quickly warmed up for breakfast.

STANELY WOOD
Oboe

Serves 6   Korean Style Barbecued Meat

*2 lb.   thinly sliced raw meat, such as chuck   ¼ tsp.   M.S.G. (optional)

Marinade: 1 tsp.   minced garlic
    ¾ cup   Japanese or light soya sauce   1 tsp.   fresh ginger, peeled and crushed
    ¼ cup   water   † 1½ tsp.   roasted sesame seeds
  ½ - ⅔ cup   sugar, to taste   1 Tblsp.   sesame seed oil
    ½ tsp.   black pepper   2   scallions, finely chopped

1. In a large glass bowl, mix soya sauce and water, and completely dissolve sugar in it.
2. Add all other ingredients for marinade and stir until well mixed.
3. Add meat, making sure it is all well coated with marinade.
4. Keep basting meat 2 - 3 hours while it marinates.
5. Cook meat slice by slice on hibachi or barbecue, turning meat only once. Serve with plain rice.

  *Meat: To slice thinly, freeze slightly, or buy already cut in Korean food store. Ask for sliced Bul-Go-Gi meat.
  †Sesame Seeds: To roast, put seeds in hot skillet with nothing added, and stir until seeds pop. Grind seeds in
      mortar or food processor until about half of them are ground to powder, leaving some seeds whole.

This recipe can also be used for braising ribs. Cut into separate ribs. Make slits down to the bone in each
rib, so they remain intact. Marinate and cook as in Bul-Go-Gi recipe. Braising ribs can be cooked by broiling
in oven, but chuck meat is best barbecued.

*Korean-born Yoon Im Chang has chosen one of her country's favourite dishes, Bul-Go-Gi, and adapted it to the
Canadian barbecue. "In Korea it is cooked to individual taste on a grill in the centre of the table. Here it can
be cooked equally well on hibachi or barbecue and served with rice and vegetables. The Spinach recipe (p. 99)
would go well with it."*

*Since Yoon's father was with the Korean foreign service, she travelled widely before obtaining her Bachelor of
Music degree from the University of Toronto. She joined the violin section of The Toronto Symphony in 1978.*

YOON IM CHANG
Violin

Serves 6

2 lb.	beef ribs (braising ribs cut in slices)

Sauce:

1 cup	tomato ketchup	1 tsp.	Worcestershire sauce
¼ cup	vinegar	2 Tblsp.	prepared mustard
⅓ cup	honey	¼ cup	hot water
½ Tblsp.	soya sauce	¼ cup	cold water
½ Tblsp.	garlic powder	1 Tblsp.	cornstarch

1. Boil ribs in water for 30 minutes. Pour off water.
2. Cook ingredients for sauce for 5 minutes.
3. Make a mixture of cold water and cornstarch, and add to sauce.
4. Pour over ribs and marinate for 24 hours.
5. Set oven to 300° F.
6. Bake for 1 hour in a covered dish. Stir mixture several times during cooking.

Violinist Jacob Groob does not cook, he confesses, because his wife, Fini, is a superb cook. He has contributed some of her favourite recipes.

During his twenty-five-year career with The Toronto Symphony, Jacob Groob has found time to play with the Baroque Quartet and the Toronto Chamber Orchestra, to conduct the Oshawa Symphony for five years, and to found the Toronto Youth Symphony, which he took on tour to Switzerland.

JACOB GROOB
Violin

Serves 4 - 6

2 lb.	ribs	1	large can tomatoes
	flour and seasoning for dredging ribs	¼ tsp.	cinnamon
	oil		nutmeg
1	large onion, chopped	1 heaping tsp.	brown sugar
1 - 2	cloves garlic, crushed		oregano (optional)
2	ribs celery, chopped	1 tsp.	salt, or to taste
		1	large handful raisins
			chopped parsley (optional)

1. Dredge ribs in flour and seasonings. Heat a little oil in heavy pan.
2. Brown ribs in oil.
3. Remove ribs from pan onto a plate.
4. Sauté onion, crushed garlic, celery until lightly browned.
5. Return ribs to pan. Add tomatoes, cinnamon, nutmeg, sugar, oregano, and salt to taste.
6. Simmer 1 hour. Add raisins and continue cooking until ribs are tender. Add parsley.

Serve over rice with a green salad on the side.

Percussionist Ray Reilly, a Torontonian, received his musical training in Toronto, New York, and Boston with private teachers. After freelancing in radio and television and with the National Ballet orchestra, he joined The Toronto Symphony in 1967. Although he likes the drums best, he finds the other percussion instruments interesting and challenging.

RAYMOND REILLY
Percussion

Serves 4 - 6

1 lb.	ground beef		1 tsp.	sugar
½ lb.	ground pork		¼ tsp.	pepper
½ cup	dry bread crumbs		½ tsp.	allspice
½ cup	milk		¼ cup	butter or drippings
1	egg, slightly beaten		2 Tblsp.	flour
1 Tblsp.	chopped onion		1½ cups	milk and cream
1 tsp.	salt			

1. Combine beef, pork, bread crumbs, milk, egg, onion, and seasonings. Shape into small balls and brown in butter or drippings, shaking skillet frequently.
2. Cover pan tightly and steam for about 15 minutes.
3. Remove meatballs from skillet with slotted spoon, and make a gravy in pan by blending in flour.
4. Add milk and cream and cook until thickened, stirring constantly. Adjust seasonings.

I double or quadruple this recipe for parties and keep the meatballs warm in the gravy. Gravy can also be served on the side. In any case, they never last long!

Audrey King describes herself as an obsessive cook; she likes to cook just about everything. An enthusiastic gardener, she also enjoys growing her own vegetables. All of her recipes included in this book come from her mother.

Seattle-born Audrey plays in the cello section of The Toronto Symphony and is a founding member of the St. Andrew's Concert Baroque Trio.

AUDREY KING
Violoncello

Serves 4 - 6

1¼ lb.	scallopini-type veal, cut into 12 pieces and pounded flat
12	paper-thin slices prosciutto ham

Stuffing:

1	garlic clove, pressed
2 Tblsp.	olive oil
2 Tblsp.	butter
3	green onions, including tops, chopped fine
10	medium mushrooms, chopped fine
1	large piece of Italian bread, soaked in milk, then squeezed out and broken up
3 Tblsp.	grated Parmesan cheese
½ cup	coarsely grated provolone or any other hard Italian-sounding kind of cheese
1 Tblsp.	chopped parsley or 4 fresh sage leaves, chopped
1	egg
	salt and pepper to taste
½ cup	chicken stock
¼ cup	brandy

1. To make the stuffing, sauté garlic in mixture of olive oil and butter until brown.
2. Remove garlic and add chopped onion and mushrooms. Sauté until limp.
3. Remove and combine onion and mushroom mixture with the squeezed bread and grated cheeses.
4. Add either parsley or sage, beaten egg, and salt and pepper to taste.
5. Place one piece of prosciutto ham on each piece of veal and a dab of stuffing on each one. Spread the stuffing flat; then roll up and secure with a toothpick.
6. Dust the rolls with flour and brown them in pan, adding more butter and oil as needed.
7. When browned, remove rolls, add the chicken stock and brandy to pan. Bring to a boil, scraping the pan. On boiling, immediately adjust heat to low; return rolls to pan, cover, and simmer for approximately 12 minutes, turning rolls once.
8. Remove rolls and place in serving dish. Keep them warm while reducing remaining sauce until it is "a little thick". Pour over rolls and serve.

NANCICAROLE (Corkie) MONOHAN
Double Bass

Serves 4

1 lb.	stewing veal, cut into sliver-thin slices, maximum 1/16 inch thick (I suggest you have your butcher do it, as it takes a great deal of patience.)	4 Tblsp.	butter or margarine
		4 Tblsp.	vegetable oil
			juice of 1/2 lemon
	salt to taste	2 cups	fresh mushrooms, sliced
	freshly ground pepper to taste	1/2 cup	cream
1 Tblsp.	flour	1/4 cup	sherry

1. Set oven to 200° F.
2. Dip veal in flour, salt, and pepper mixture.
3. In heavy skillet, heat butter and oil over high heat. Cook veal, tossing constantly until it looks done. This has to be done quickly or veal will be tough.
4. Place veal on platter, sprinkle with lemon juice, and keep warm in oven.
5. Pour off most of remaining fat in skillet. Add mushrooms and cook for 3 to 4 minutes over medium heat.
6. Pour in cream and bring to boil. Be sure to stir in any brown bits that cling to pan. Cream will thicken, but if too pasty looking, add a little prepared cooking sauce.
7. Pour over veal and mix through. Should sauce be too thick or even too bland, add sherry just before serving.

Serve over egg noodles or steamed rice.

HUBERT MEYER
Tuba

Serves 6 to 8, depending on the size of the leg of lamb

1	leg of lamb, fresh or frozen	olive oil
	salt, pepper, rosemary leaves	red wine
2-3	cloves garlic, minced	

1. Remove all fat from the leg and then remove the bone, leaving only the shank bone for easier handling on the barbecue.
2. Salt the meat, add some coarse ground pepper, and rub in the minced garlic.
3. Add rosemary leaves generously and cover the meat with approximately 2 Tblsp. of olive oil.
4. Add at least one medium-size glass of red wine.
5. Turn the meat 2 to 3 times per day in the marinade and let it marinate for about 2 days.
6. When the barbecue fire (or oven) is at an initial temperature of 375° - 450° F., barbecue lamb like steak, approximately 20 minutes each side. Sprinkle the meat with the remaining marinade while it is cooking.

Serve with fresh green onions and warm French bread or boiled vegetables and potatoes.

Richly marinated lamb turning slowly on a spit is a delight that Dr. Jan Matejcek remembers from tales his father told him of pre-World War I Bosnia and from his own Czechoslovakian childhood. In Canada, he has adapted his love of lamb to our outdoor barbecues.

A composer and pianist, Jan Matejcek has been associated with the Canadian music scene since coming to this country. Formerly Director of the Ontario Federation of Symphony Orchestras and of the Ontario Choral Federation, he is presently Vice-President and Managing Director of Performing Rights Organization of Canada Limited.

Dr. JAN MATEJCEK
Composer and Pianist

Serves 4 - 6

1-1½ lb.	lamb shoulder or leg	2 Tblsp.	fat
1	large onion	2 cups	long grain rice (not converted)
1	medium carrot		salt and pepper

1. Cut lamb into small inch-square pieces.
2. Finely chop the onion and carrot.
3. Melt fat in a dutch oven; brown meat and vegetables.
4. Add enough water so that contents of pan will not burn. Simmer gently for approximately 1 hour or until meat is tender, adding water as necessary.
5. Bring 3 cups water to the boil. Remove meat from heat. Place rice on top of meat. *Do not mix with lamb.*
6. Pour boiling water over meat and rice; return pan to heat and cover. Cook approximately 20 minutes.
7. As the rice cooks and water disappears, make holes in the rice and add more water.
8. Cook a further 15 - 20 minutes.
9. Check seasoning and correct if necessary.

This dish is best made an hour in advance of serving and kept warm.

Pilaf Boltyansky is only one of his mother's dishes that Russian-born Eduard Boltyansky likes to make. "I like to cook," he confides, "and not just Russian. I am learning Canadian cooking, too."

Eduard Boltyansky received his musical training in Russia and performed with the orchestra of the Bolshoi Ballet and the Moscow Philharmonic before coming to Canada in 1974. After a year with the National Ballet orchestra, he joined The Toronto Symphony in 1975.

EDUARD BOLTYANSKY
Viola

Serves 10 - 12   Potted Meat

3 lb.	lean veal, with bone		1 tsp.	ginger
3 lb.	lean lamb, with bone		1 tsp.	allspice
2	large onions		2 Tblsp.	salt
1 tsp.	pepper			

1. Place lamb and veal in a large pot and fill with enough water to cover meat. Boil for three hours. Cool.
2. Take the meat off the bones and put through a grinder with the onions and spices.
3. Place meat mixture back into meat juices and boil for 25 - 35 minutes.
4. Pour into meat loaf pan and chill.
5. Cut into thin slices.

PEARL PALMASON
Violin

Serves 4

2 lb.	lean fresh pork butt or shoulder		¼ cup	chopped green pepper
2 Tblsp.	vegetable oil		½ cup	chopped celery
2	medium onions, sliced		1 tsp.	chili powder or to taste
1 14-oz.	can tomatoes		1 tsp.	salt

1. Cut pork in cubes. Heat the oil in a heavy frying pan or skillet.
2. Brown pork and sliced onions, stirring well.
3. Add all other ingredients. Stir well.
4. Cover and simmer for 1 hour over a gentle heat.
5. Season to taste.

   Serve with boiled rice or mashed potatoes and Hot Red Cabbage Salad (p. 108).

BERNARD TEMOIN
Bass Clarinet

Serves 2 - 4

2	or more boiled potatoes		1 lb.	sauerkraut or ½ lb. sauerkraut and
½ lb.	bacon, or as much as you want			½ medium head of lightly cooked cabbage
2	onions, chopped			peppercorns
2	pork chops		½ bottle	good beer
	butter		1 or 2	peeled tomatoes
1	big kielbasa (Polish sausage), sliced			salt

1. Boil potatoes in their skins until three-quarters done. Peel and chop into big pieces.
2. Chop bacon into large pieces. Fry in a large skillet. Remove to a small bowl.
3. Fry onions until lightly browned. Remove to a large bowl.
4. Fry pork chops quickly until just brown. Place with onions.
5. Fry potatoes in remaining fat and place with chops and onions.
6. Add a little butter to pan and fry the sliced sausage.
7. Drain and rinse sauerkraut. Place it, or the half and half mixture of sauerkraut and cabbage, plus a few peppercorns in a casserole or big pot and heat.
8. When mixture is simmering, pour in beer and then tomatoes (whole or chopped in quarters). Simmer 2 or 3 minutes. Add salt and simmer for 1 hour. Check seasoning.

Guest pianist Janina Fialkowska acquired this Polish recipe from her aunt — " a fabulous cook, like all Polish women!" Janina first ate bigos in Poland as it was prepared by the peasants in the Carpathians and kept on ordering it whenever she was on tour in that country. "Because I also love Alsatian choucroute garni, I've combined the best from both recipes and have come up with my own version, Bigos Fialkowska."

Montreal-born, Janina studied at the École De Musique Vincent D'Indy and at the University of Montreal, in Paris, and at the Juilliard School of Music in New York. She has performed with the Israel Philharmonic as well as with major orchestras across the United States and in Canada.

JANINA FIALKOWSKA
Piano — Guest Artist

Serves 4 - 5

2-3 lb.	piece "country style" ribs	¼ cup	French dressing
	pepper and seasoned salt	2 Tblsp.	salad oil
¾ cup	ketchup		few shakes of Tabasco sauce
½ cup	pineapple marmalade		

1. Set oven to 375° F.
2. Rub a generous amount of pepper and seasoned salt into the lean surfaces of the meat.
3. Place ribs fat side up in a lightly oiled, shallow baking pan.
4. Roast for 30 minutes and turn.
5. Brush ribs with a mixture of the remaining ingredients and bake at 325° F. for 2 hours or until done, brushing with sauce and turning every 20 - 30 minutes.
6. Slice and serve.

   If the ribs are to be frozen and used later, reduce baking time to 1½ hours. Reheat for 35 minutes at 375° F.

GEORGINA ROBERTS
Violoncello

Serves 4

2 lb.	spareribs, very meaty (Ask butcher to cut bones.)		2 Tblsp.	catsup
¼ cup	boiling water		¼ tsp.	cloves
1	beef bouillon cube		¼-½ tsp.	pepper
1½ tsp.	garlic salt		2 Tblsp.	cooking oil

1. Set oven to 325° F.
2. Dissolve beef cube in boiling water.
3. Stir in remaining ingredients.
4. Brush sauce on both sides of ribs.
5. Bake for 1½ hours, turning and basting ribs.

Jean and David Wulkan, a husband-and-wife team, met in the violin section of The Toronto Symphony. David was born in Berlin and came to the TS in 1952 after studying in Israel and at the Guildhall School of Music in England. Jean, a Torontonian, graduated from the Royal Conservatory of Music in Toronto and the Meadowmount School of Music in New York before joining the orchestra in 1964. She has formed a trio which plays in schools, libraries, and hospitals; David plays in a string quartet.

Outside of music, the creativity of this couple is expressed in different ways. "I love to cook," says Jean, "and David loves to make fine furniture."

JEAN WULKAN
Violin

Serves 4

2 lb.	side or back spareribs		2 Tblsp.	soya sauce
2 10-oz.	cans consommé			green peppers and onion (optional)
2 Tblsp.	brown sugar			

1. Brown the ribs and marinate them in mixture of remaining ingredients for 24 hours.
2. Set oven to 375° F.
3. Cook the ribs in the mixture for 1 hour.

   Serve with rice and tossed salad and cheese rolls.

Cooking is a hobby which trombonist Frank Reynolds and his wife both share.

Frank began studying the trombone in his teens in Brockville and later in Toronto with Harry Hawe, then TS principal trombonist. During World War II, he went overseas with an orchestra, led by Bert Niosi, to entertain the armed forces. After his return Frank freelanced in opera and ballet orchestras, and then joined The Toronto Symphony in 1967. For many years he has been playing in Symphony Street, a children's music education program given in public libraries on Saturday mornings. He is a member of a quartet called The Sounds of Brass.

FRANK REYNOLDS
Trombone

Serves 4

2 Tblsp. salt	white pepper
¼ cup olive oil	pasta *aglio olio* (see below)
1 lb. beef liver, very thinly sliced	

1. Heat a large cast-iron skillet until very hot (dry); sprinkle with salt and add olive oil.
2. Add beef liver, one slice at a time, turning immediately. Remove liver from pan and drain on paper towel.
3. Sprinkle pepper lightly over liver.

Serve with pasta *aglio olio,* a green salad, and a light red wine.

PASTA AGLIO OLIO

1 lb. pasta, cooked	1 or 2 cloves garlic
	2-4 Tblsp. olive oil

1. Sauté garlic cloves in oil.
2. Remove garlic.
3. Add oil to hot, cooked pasta.
4. Toss until pasta is well coated.

THOMAS MONOHAN
Principal Double Bass

Serves 4 - 6   Liver Meat Loaf

1 cup	oatmeal		1 tsp.	brown sugar
¾ cup	whole wheat flour or ¼ cup		1½-2 cups	milk
	Vita B and ¼ cup bran		1 lb.	beef liver
2 tsp.	salt		½ lb.	suet from a fresh beef kidney

1. Set oven to 300° F.
2. Mix dry ingredients and add milk. Let mixture stand.
3. Put skinned liver and half of suet through the blender.
4. Cube other half of suet.
5. Mix everything together and turn into a buttered casserole. Cover with foil.
6. Place casserole in a pan of warm water in the oven and bake for 2 hours.

VARIATIONS: Substitute kidney for liver, or use half and half. Substitute ground beef, veal, lamb, or pork, plus chopped onion or crumbled bacon for any amount of liver desired.

PEARL PALMASON
Violin

Serves 4 - 6

3 pairs	veal sweetbreads	4 Tblsp.	butter
2 Tblsp.	lemon juice	4 Tblsp.	flour
1	stalk celery	1 cup	light cream
½ cup	chopped onion	1	chicken breast, cooked and chopped
1 tsp.	salt	½ cup	diced ham
	pepper to taste	¼ cup	black olives, sliced

1. Clean and rinse sweetbreads thoroughly, and soak in cold water for 3-4 hours.
2. Boil sweetbreads with lemon juice, celery, onion, salt, and pepper in enough water to cover for 20 minutes.
3. Drain, reserving liquid.
4. Remove membranes and cut sweetbreads into small cubes.
5. Melt butter; stir in flour.
6. Gradually add stock from sweetbreads and cream, stirring until smooth.
7. Add chicken, diced ham, and chopped olives.
8. Simmer for 5 minutes.

Serve on noodles.

COROL McCARTNEY
Violin

Serves 4

1	set of calves' brains (about 1 lb.)	3 or 4	eggs
	salt		butter or margarine
1	medium onion, chopped	1 cup	sliced mushrooms (optional)

1. Rinse brains with cold water. Put in a bowl with salted cold water and soak for about an hour. Pour off water and then remove thin layer of skin from brains.
2. Simmer brains in boiling salted water for about 18 minutes. Drain and cut into small pieces.
3. Sauté chopped onion in butter or margarine until golden. (If using mushrooms, add to cooked onion.) Add the brains and stir with onion. Beat eggs slightly and add to mixture, stirring until eggs are cooked and resemble scrambled eggs.

May be served as an appetizer with a small salad or as a main course luncheon with baked potato and salad.

During his more than fifty years with the Symphony — he joined at the age of seventeen in the days of Dr. von Kunits — Berul Sugarman has firmly established himself in Toronto's musical life. He has taught in schools, performed in a dance orchestra, and at one time formed his own string quartet, the Galant Chamber Music Players. Today, he enjoys playing the gamba with a group of gamba-playing friends.

BERUL SUGARMAN
Violin

Serves 4 - 6

Pastry for Double Crust Pie:

1½ cups	all-purpose flour
½ tsp.	salt
½ cup	shortening (mixture of 1 Tblsp. butter and remainder lard is recommended)
5-6 Tblsp.	water

Filling:

1 lb.	ground beef (or ¾ lb. beef and ¼ lb. ground pork)
½ cup	chopped onion
2	zucchini squash, unpeeled and chopped (approximately 1½ cups)
1 cup	fresh or canned tomatoes, seeded, peeled, and coarsely chopped
1-2 tsp.	basil (This should be the dominant flavour.)
dash	garlic powder

1. Sift together dry ingredients and cut shortening finely into mixture. Add water slowly, tossing gently with fork. Form ball, knead lightly, cut dough in half. Wrap the two halves in waxed paper and chill for 30 minutes.
2. Set oven to 350° F.
3. Brown meat in skillet; add onion and cook until soft. Add tomatoes and zucchini. (Don't overcook the zucchini.) Add seasonings.
4. Roll out dough and line 9-inch pie plate.
5. Pour mixture into lined pie plate and cover with top crust. Crimp the edges together to keep in juices. Slit top to allow steam to escape.
6. Bake in preheated oven for 45 minutes, or until crust is golden brown. Let cool slightly before serving.

Henry Ingram, whose distinguished tenor voice has delighted Toronto Symphony listeners on several occasions, describes himself as a self-taught cook who enjoys eating what he cooks. He says of his Basil 'N' Beef Pie, "an exciting combination, with basil the unexpected accent." He also claims to make a "terrific" scrambled egg and bacon sandwich for eating when he is in a hurry.

Henry received much of his training in the Opera Division of the University of Toronto's Faculty of Music on a scholarship which he won while he was a student at Florida State University. In recent years he has performed with the Canadian Opera Company.

HENRY INGRAM
Tenor — Guest Artist

Serves 6 - 8

2	medium cabbages	½ cup	chopped parsley
2	large onions, finely chopped	½ tsp.	pepper
¼ cup	oil	1 Tblsp.	salt
1 cup	rice	1 14-oz.	can tomato sauce
¾ lb.	ground beef	2 Tblsp.	oil
½ lb.	ground pork		

1. Set oven to 400° F.
2. Steam cabbage until soft enough to peel off leaves.
3. Sauté onions in oil.
4. Boil rice until tender.
5. When rice is ready, cool and mix thoroughly with onions, meat, and seasonings.
6. Fill each cabbage leaf with about 1 tablespoonful of the mixture. (Large leaves can be halved, cutting from top to bottom.) Fold in an envelope shape and roll tightly, placing cabbage rolls in a large pot or casserole.
7. Bring tomato sauce to boil, adding oil. Pour over cabbage rolls and bake tightly covered for 30 minutes. Reduce oven temperature to 350° F. and bake 30 minutes longer.

JULIAN KOLKOWKSI
Violin

Serves 3 - 4

3	acorn squash (Choose green ones with a touch of yellow.)	1 tsp.	parsley (or sage)
6 Tblsp.	honey	1 lb.	mild pork sausage meat
1 tsp.	salt		bread crumbs

1. Set oven to 350° F.
2. Wash and halve squash. Remove strings and seeds.
3. Put 1 Tblsp. honey in each half.
4. Sprinkle salt and parsley (or sage) over the squash.
5. Fill the squash cavity with the sausage meat and top with bread crumbs.
6. Put on rack in roaster and add 1 inch of water to bottom of pan.
7. Bake covered for 40 minutes. Uncover and bake 10 minutes longer, or until brown.

Paul Meyer's stuffed squash recipe came from his great-aunt in St. Louis.

Paul was born in Kentucky and studied music at the University of Illinois and Indiana University. He also spent five summers at the Banff School of Fine Arts, then moved to Toronto to play with the Galliard Ensemble for one year before joining the TS in 1979.

PAUL MEYER
Violin

Serves 4 - 6

1-1½ lb.	beef (round or chuck steak)		6-8 oz.	tomato paste
1	clove garlic		6-8 oz.	water
2 Tblsp.	chili powder		½ - ⅔ cup	chopped onions
¼-½ tsp.	Tabasco		1 cup	Jack cheese (Cheddar in emergency)
1 tsp.	salt		1 cup	shredded lettuce
2	sprigs parsley, chopped		2	tomatoes, diced or chopped

1. Sear meat on both sides. Slice fat off the meat and rub it on hot griddle or pot.
2. Cook meat in a covered pan until very well done, and easily shredded, together with garlic, chili powder, Tabasco, salt, parsley, tomato paste, and water. Simmer until excess water has dissipated. (Do not cover too tightly or no evaporation will take place.)
3. Shred the meat.
4. Drain any remaining moisture away. Fill Tortillas (p. 87) with meat.

Serve with separate bowls of chopped onions, grated cheese, shredded lettuce, and chopped or diced tomatoes. Tacos can also be served with Guacamole (p.12). We've also made a vegetarian version using soya burger instead of beef. Gene Watts loves it!.

1 cup	**flour**		**2 Tblsp.**	**shortening**
½ cup	**corn meal**		**⅓ cup**	**(or more) warm water**
½ tsp.	**salt**			

1. If you own a food processor, put all ingredients together (you might have to do a bit at a time) and blend as dough. If no food processor is at hand, use your hands.
2. When dough is formed, roll little balls (10 or 11) into pancakes 6 or 7 inches in diameter.
3. Fling the pancakes on a hot greased griddle. When they are almost crisp, fold in half. Fill them with prepared shredded beef (p. 86) and toss back on griddle until crisp.

Extra tortillas can be less crisply fried to be steamed later and eaten buttered and salted, or they can be extremely crisply fried and broken up to make dip chips.

Serves 4 - 5   Family Casserole

1½ cups	macaroni			salt, pepper, spices to taste
1 lb.	ground beef		¼ cup	water
1	onion, grated		1 cup	grated Cheddar cheese
1	egg		½-1 cup	tomato juice
6	crackers, crumbled			

1. Set oven to 325° F.
2. Cook macaroni in boiling, salted water. Drain well.
3. Mix beef, onion, egg, cracker crumbs, seasonings, and water.
4. Lightly oil casserole.
5. To assemble, layer grated cheese, half the macaroni, more grated cheese, beef mixture, tomato juice, remaining macaroni, remaining cheese.
6. Bake for 2½ hours.

Patricia Krueger, busy mother of two young sons, has chosen a quick and easy recipe for the working mother and one that is very popular with her family.

Patricia grew up in Toronto in a musical household. Her father was Harvey Perrin, well known in the music education field and Director of Music with the Toronto Board of Education. He was also the initiator of the Junior Women's Committee's Prelude Concerts. Patricia began her training in percussion with the orchestra of Lawrence Park Collegiate. A member of the TS since 1960, she enjoys her double role as keyboard player and percussionist. She performs on the piano, organ, celeste, and harpsichord, and a bewildering array of percussion instruments such as the tam-tam, ratchet, slapsticks, wood-block, chimes, cymbals, glockenspiel, triangle, xylophone, and drums.

PATRICIA KRUEGER
Keyboard and Percussion

Serves 6 hungry or 9 careful eaters

1 lb. lasagna noodles	salt, pepper, onion powder, oregano to taste
1 large green pepper, finely chopped	1 28-oz. can tomato sauce
oil	1 pint cottage cheese
2 lb. ground beef	12 oz. Mozzarella cheese, sliced or grated
1 can mushroom pieces	

1. Cook lasagna noodles in salted water until almost tender, about 10 minutes. Remove from heat, drain, and rinse in cold water. Separate noodles and spread to cool.
2. In a large frypan sauté green pepper in a little oil until tender. Set aside.
3. Sauté ground beef without browning. Drain off fat and combine beef and green pepper.
4. Drain mushrooms and add to meat and green pepper mixture.
5. Season with salt, pepper, onion powder, and oregano.
6. Set oven to 350° F.
7. Butter a 13 x 9 x 2-inch pan. Arrange lasagna noodles lengthwise, 3 to a layer, cutting to fit the pan.
8. Arrange in alternating layers the noodles, meat mixture (spooning), tomato sauce (without oozing), cottage cheese (spooning), Mozzarella cheese.
9. Repeat each layer 3 times, ending with a layer of noodles.
10. Put remaining Mozzarella cheese on top. Cover well with foil. Bake for 40 minutes.

Reserve some sauce to serve with individual portions. Serve with green salad, garlic bread, and red Italian wine.

Torontonian Teresa Obercian began her musical career with that early nurturer of fine musicians, the Lawrence Park Collegiate Orchestra. She followed this with violin study at the Royal Conservatory of Music, at Laval University in Quebec, and in Geneva. She joined The Toronto Symphony in 1956, the first year of Conductor Walter Susskind's tenure. Today, in addition to her TS life, she plays occasionally with the Pro Arte Orchestra.

TERESA OBERCIAN
Violin

Serves 8

2 cups	flour	1 tsp.	salt
2	eggs	1 Tblsp.	oil
4	egg whites		

1. Blend all ingredients by hand or in food processor.
2. Roll out and dust with flour to proper consistency for pasta machine (not too wet or too dry).
3. Make desired noodle through pasta machine and hang to separate until ready for use.

TS husband-and-wife team Joe Umbrico and Judy Loman met at the Curtis Institute in Philadelphia and transplanted their talents to Toronto in 1957. Today, they make music, teach, Judy records, and they both cook.

The extra egg whites in Joe's pasta were a happy accident and give a lighter-than-usual texture. The southern Italian casserole Taiella (p. 104) was acquired from Joe's aunt.

JOSEPH UMBRICO
Principal Trumpet

Serves 2 - 3

⅓ cup	olive oil		½ lb.	cooked seafood — clams, scallops, chopped squid, shrimp, etc.
2	garlic cloves, finely chopped		¾ lb.	pasta
1	medium onion, finely chopped			grated Romano cheese
1	small green pepper, finely chopped			chili peppers, crushed
1 cup	white wine			
½ cup	bottled clam juice			

1. In a large cast-iron skillet, heat olive oil.
2. Add garlic, onion, and green pepper. Saute until soft. Remove from pan. Reserve liquid.
3. Add white wine and clam juice. Bring to boil; add seafood and sautéed vegetables.
4. Mix and pour over boiled, drained pasta.
5. Add grated Romano cheese and chili peppers to taste.

   Serve with a salad of Rucola (an Italian lettuce) and radishes with a tart dressing, and a well chilled Verdicchio.

THOMAS MONOHAN
Double Bass

Serves 3 - 4

2 cups	fresh basil (not too tightly packed)	1 tsp.	salt
½ cup	olive oil	½ cup	freshly grated Parmesan cheese
2 Tblsp.	pine nuts (pignoli)	2 Tblsp.	freshly grated Romano cheese
2	cloves garlic, peeled and lightly crushed		softened butter
			hot cooked pasta

1. Mix first five ingredients together at high speed in a blender, stopping occasionally to scrape the sides of the blender with a spatula.
2. Pour mixture into a mixing bowl and beat into the pesto the cheeses and several tablespoons of softened butter.
3. Spoon a few dollops over any variety of hot cooked pasta

A native of Baltimore, John Aler has sung with numerous opera companies and has performed as soloist with many symphony orchestras and at summer festivals throughout the United States and Europe.

John writes: "This recipe is a favourite of mine. It is a seasonal dish as it requires fresh basil, available only in summer. However, the anticipation throughout a long winter of a wonderful pesto makes it that much better. This mixture used to be ground with a pestle (pesto). It's a simple dish and makes a very fine first course or a delicious lunch."

JOHN ALER
Tenor — Guest Artist

Serves 4

8 oz.	Swiss cheese — Emmenthaler		1½ cups	dry white wine (Étoile du Valais)
8 oz.	Swiss Cheese — Gruyère			pepper and salt
2½ Tblsp.	flour		3 Tblsp.	kirsch
	garlic			crusty French bread in cubes

1. Grate cheese (not too fine) and mix in flour.
2. Rub chafing dish with garlic.
3. Heat wine in dish over medium flame. As soon as wine starts to bubble (do not bring to a boil), add cheese bit by bit; stir *allegretto* with wooden spoon.
4. Keep mixture bubbling; add pepper and salt to taste, and kirsch.
5. Transfer to fondue burner on table; keep stirring.
6. Spear cubes of bread and dip into fondue. Regulate alcohol flame under dish. Heat must be steady, but not too hot.

   Serve with green salad or raw carrots and celery, and fruit salad for dessert.

Mario Duschenes has sent this note with his recipe for Cheese Fondue. "Since my wife is the world's greatest cook, I feel totally inadequate in the kitchen. The only dish my family accepts with enthusiasm when I do the cooking is my own cheese fondue — a souvenir of my years as a student at the Geneva Conservatory. Cheese fondue is not just another meal, but the kind of meal you like to share with good friends who all eat out of the same bowl. This usually creates a very friendly and jolly atmosphere around the table, especially in front of a fire after a day of skiing. I only hate washing up. The cheese sticks to everything."

A flutist, with many recordings to his credit, Mario Duschenes is now a professor at McGill University and Music Director of Youth Concerts of the Montreal, Quebec, and Vancouver Symphony Orchestras. He has conducted The Toronto Symphony Young People's Concerts, as well as a series of special Public School Concerts for students in Grades 7 and 8, at Massey Hall.

MARIO DUSCHENES
Guest Conductor

. . . the first concerts given by the New Symphony Orchestra were called "Twilight Concerts"? They ran from 5:15 to 6:15 p.m. to catch the office crowd and to allow the musicians to get to their theatres for the evening performance.

. . . "Twilight Concerts" lasted until 1932 when "talkies" came in and players were freed for evening concerts?

. . . the New Symphony Orchestra's first concert was on April 23, 1923 and the program read: "Overture to 'Der Freischutz' — Weber; Slavonic Dance — Dvorak; Two Hungarian Dances — Brahms; Symphony No. 5 in E Minor — Tchaikowsky"?

. . . approximately 60 musicians played in the New Symphony Orchestra's first season with a budget of $5000 and that the orchestra today numbers 100 with an annual budget in the millions?

. . . the Symphony's first woman member was harpist Muriel Donnellan, who joined in the 1923/24 season? Today women comprise 25 per cent of the full orchestra.

Serves 6

6   artichokes
juice of 1 lemon

Sauce: Yield 1½ cups

3   egg yolks
3 Tblsp.   lemon juice
1¼ tsp.   arrowroot

¾ tsp.   salt
1¼ cups   cold chicken broth
salt and white pepper

1. Prepare artichokes. Pull off tough outer leaves — about 1 row. Cut off the stems and top quarter of each artichoke. Trim sharp tips of leaves with scissors. Trim the base. Drop the artichokes into a kettle of salted, cold water acidulated with juice of lemon.
2. Cover with cheesecloth and bring to a boil. Simmer 30 minutes or until bottoms are tender.
3. Transfer artichokes to a rack and allow to drain upside down until cool enough to handle. Spread leaves apart and pull out centres. Remove chokes with a spoon.
4. In a small stainless steel, or enamelled, pan, whisk together yolks, lemon juice, arrowroot, and salt. Whisk in broth in a stream. Cook over gentle heat, stirring well until sauce is thickened. Season to taste.
5. While artichokes are warm, arrange on plates. To serve, fill with *avgolemono* sauce.

DANIEL RUDDICK
Percussion

Serves 4 - 6

2 lb.	Brussels sprouts
4 Tblsp.	butter
1 Tblsp.	oil
1	large onion, finely chopped
½ cup	finely chopped fresh mushrooms

	salt and pepper to taste
pinch	nutmeg
	juice of 1 lemon
½ cup	broken pecans or walnuts

1. Cook sprouts in boiling salted water about 5 minutes, or until firm but not soft.
2. In skillet melt 2 Tblsp. butter with 1 Tblsp. oil. Add onion; cook over medium heat with lid on for 2 or 3 minutes, shaking pan occasionally.
3. Add mushrooms, salt, pepper, and nutmeg.
4. Lower heat; cook a further 5 minutes, shaking pan often.
5. Add lemon juice and rest of measured butter.
6. Mix well. Pour over drained sprouts and serve sprinkled with chopped pecans or walnuts.

JEAN AND DAVID WULKAN
Violins

Serves 4 - 6

1	red cabbage	**¾-1 cup**	wine vinegar
3-4 Tblsp.	Speck (a type of smoked pork fat available at German or Dutch delicatessens. This is essential for the final flavour.)		salt to taste freshly ground pepper to taste
		2	cooking apples, unpeeled, quartered, and cored
2	onions, quartered	**6**	cloves, tied in a cheesecloth bag
½-¾ cup	sugar		

1. After removing outer leaves, cut cabbage into quarters; core and slice.
2. In a large saucepan, or dutch oven, melt the finely cut *Speck*. Sauté the cabbage.
3. Add onions, sugar, wine vinegar, salt, pepper, and apples.
4. Stir all together. Add cloves. Cook over medium heat about 1 hour, or until tender. Remove cloves.

This can be cooked and frozen. The measurements and quantities are approximate, according to the size of the red cabbage. If there is too much vinegar, add a little sugar, and vice versa.

HUBERT MEYER
Tuba

Serves 4

1 10-oz.	package fresh spinach			salt to taste
1 tsp.	light soya sauce		1 tsp.	white vinegar
¼ tsp.	minced garlic		dash	paprika
1 Tblsp.	chopped scallion (green onion)		1 tsp.	roasted sesame seeds (See p. 65.)
½ tsp.	fresh ginger, peeled and crushed		½ tsp.	sesame oil
	black pepper to taste			

1. Into boiling water put washed spinach to scald it. Remove pot immediately from heat. Drain spinach. Rinse with cold water. Squeeze out all water completely.
2. Cut resulting ball of spinach into 3 pieces.
3. Shake spinach loose into a bowl.
4. Add soya sauce, mixing well by hand.
5. Add all other ingredients and mix well.

Instead of spinach, bean sprouts or green beans may be used. Serve cold with rice cooked according to taste.

YOON IM CHANG
Violin

Serves 4 vegetarians or 6-8 when used as a side dish with meat

6	medium sweet potatoes		1 tsp.	nutmeg
¼ cup	oil, preferably cold-pressed		2 Tblsp.	brandy or cognac
	safflower or sunflower		2 oz.	ground hazelnuts (unsalted)
2 Tblsp.	honey or maple syrup			

1. Set oven to 350° F.
2. Wash and scrub potatoes, but do not peel. Cut in half and make a few cuts on each of the freshly cut surfaces.
3. Take a glass baking dish and coat it with oil. Arrange potatoes face up in dish.
4. Heat rest of oil gently in a small pan. Add about 2 Tblsp. of honey or maple syrup and stir until as well dissolved as possible.
5. Add nutmeg, brandy or cognac, and pour about one-third over potatoes. Now sprinkle over ground nuts to make a little mound on each potato.
6. Finish by pouring (very gently) the remaining spiced sauce over the potatoes, trying not to disturb the nuts.
7. Bake about 1 hour.

   As an alternative to the ground hazelnuts, fill the bottom of the dish with whole, shelled hazelnuts after 30 minutes of baking.

Anton Kuerti is a strict vegetarian; hence his recipe for Sweet Potatoes alla Breve.

A pianist whose career has taken him around the globe, Anton Kuerti has played with virtually all of the world's great conductors. He is acclaimed for his interpretation of the piano music of Beethoven and Schubert.

ANTON KUERTI
Piano — Guest Artist

Serves 6

1½ lb.	ground beef		1 cup	grated Mozzarella or Cheddar cheese
2	large onions, chopped		1 28-oz.	can tomatoes or 2 10-oz. cans
2	stalks celery, chopped			tomato bisque soup
1	green pepper, chopped			bread crumbs
1	large eggplant, unpeeled			several small cubes of margarine

1. Set oven to 325° F.
2. Brown ground beef in frying pan.
3. Sauté chopped onions, celery, and green pepper until tender.
4. Slice eggplant into ½-inch slices.
5. To make up dish, layer the ingredients repeatedly in a large lasagna-type dish in the following order: tomatoes or soup, ground beef, sautéed vegetables, eggplant, cheese. End with cheese layers on top.
6. Sprinkle bread crumbs and small cubes of margarine on top.
7. Bake for 1 hour or until bubbly. Cover for last half of cooking time.

PATRICIA KRUEGER
Percussion and Keyboard

Serves 6   Spinach Cheese Bake

4 cups	fresh spinach, washed and chopped		6	eggs, lightly beaten
1 tsp.	salt		$\frac{1}{8}$ tsp.	black pepper
2 Tblsp.	chopped parsley		1 cup	Ricotta or Feta cheese, crumbled
6 Tblsp.	oil			

1. Set oven to 400° F.
2. Mix spinach with salt.
3. Allow to drip for 5 minutes.
4. Add parsley.
5. Pour on oil and spread in shallow baking pan.
6. Mix together eggs, pepper, and cheese.
7. Make 6 hollows or dents in spinach and pour cheese mixture into each.
8. Bake 30 minutes.

Former Principal Clarinet Avrahm Galper doesn't cook, but his wife's Spinach Cheese Bake is one of his favourites.

Born in Edmonton, musically trained in Palestine, Avrahm joined the TS in 1947 on his return to Canada. During his long and distinguished career he has written books on the clarinet. Today, retired from the orchestra because of ill health, he still teaches at the Royal Conservatory and the Faculty of Music of the University of Toronto.

AVRAHM GALPER
Former Principal Clarinet

Serves 6 - 8

2	cloves garlic, crushed		1	small eggplant, diced
2	onions, sliced		½	green pepper, cut in strips
¼ cup	butter		5	tomatoes, quartered
1 cup	stock		½ cup	seedless grapes
½ cup	olive oil		½	cauliflower, cut up
4	carrots, sliced		½	summer squash, cut up
2	potatoes, diced		2	small zucchini, diced
			½	celery root, peeled and diced

1. Sauté garlic and onions in butter.
2. Add stock and oil and then boil.
3. Pour over vegetables in casserole.
4. Cover and bake at 350° F. for 25 minutes.

Double bass player Jane McAdam arrived at The Toronto Symphony in 1968 fresh from an early start with the Lawrence Park Collegiate Institute Orchestra and the National Youth Orchestra. In off-orchestra hours she teaches privately and plays for children with the Symphony's educational programs, Symphony Street and Symphony Preludes.

Jane's casseroles won raves, she admits, when she first made them for a surprise anniversary party for her parents, and she has made them, with variations, ever since.

JANE McADAM
Double Bass

This recipe for a Tunisian vegetable stew in which an egg is poached, allows you to 'do your own thing' and amounts are to taste.

fresh or canned tomatoes	peppers, chopped
tomato paste	eggplants, chopped
cumin	zucchini, chopped
cinnamon	olive oil
honey	garlic
salt	parsley
pepper (hot)	basil
pepper (black)	eggs — one per person
onions, chopped	couscous (cracked wheat)

1. Set oven to 350° F.
2. Blanch and peel tomatoes to remove skins or use Italian plum tomatoes. Add tomato paste.
3. Place in pan and add spices to taste. Simmer.
4. Sauté chosen vegetables in plenty of olive oil, salting lightly. Add garlic, parsley, and basil.
5. Add sautéed vegetables to simmering tomatoes.
6. Lightly grease a suitable baking dish and pour in vegetable mixture.
7. Make depressions in mixture with the back of a large spoon and slide in the required number of eggs ready for poaching.

8. Bake until just firm.
9. Just before serving, prepare the couscous using a proportion of ½ cup grain to 1 cup boiling water. Stir constantly for 3 - 4 minutes until thick. Add a splash of olive oil.
10. Serve Chakchouka over couscous.

Because trombonist Gordon Sweeney and his wife are vegetarians, they are constantly on the look-out for new and interesting vegetable combinations. He likes his Chakchouka, a Tunisian vegetable stew, because of its versatility.

Texas-born, Gordon studied trombone at the Curtis Institute in Philadelphia and then returned to his home state to play in the Dallas Symphony. He joined the TS in 1974. He rejoices in the rich cultural life of Toronto — "a fine place to bring up three daughters," he says, "and also to keep a musician busy". As well as performing with The Toronto Symphony, which he proudly claims gives twice as many concerts as most well-known orchestras, he also teaches performance majors in the Faculty of Music, University of Toronto.

GORDON SWEENEY
Principal Trombone

TAIELLA

Serves 4 - 6

Vegetable Casserole

6 small zucchini	garlic (optional)
4 small potatoes	1½-2 28-oz. cans tomatoes, broken up with juice
1 medium Spanish onion	bread crumbs
fresh or dried basil	Parmesan cheese, grated
salt and pepper to taste	olive oil
celery leaves	

1. Set oven to 375° F.
2. Slice zucchini, potatoes, and onion ⅛ inch thick and combine with seasonings.
3. Spread a small amount of oil on bottom of a 4-quart casserole.
4. Start with a layer of half of the vegetable mixture. Top with a layer of half of the tomatoes and their juice. Sprinkle with a layer of bread crumbs and top with Parmesan cheese.
5. Repeat the process, using up all the vegetable mixture and tomatoes. Sprinkle with crumbs and cheese and a little olive oil.
6. Cover well. Bake in preheated oven for 45 minutes. Lower heat to 350° F. and continue cooking for another 45 minutes, or until potatoes are tender. Remove cover for last 10 minutes.

JUDY LOMAN
Harp

Serves 4 - 6

Caesar Salad

2	heads romaine lettuce
½ cup	chopped green onions or shallots
3 Tblsp.	Parmesan cheese
4	slices caraway rye bread

Dressing:

2	large garlic cloves
1½ Tblsp.	capers
7	strips anchovy fillets

1 Tblsp.	peppercorns
½ tsp.	salt
¼ tsp.	Worcestershire sauce
½ tsp.	dry mustard
	juice of 2 lemons
¾ cup	olive oil
¼ cup	wine vinegar
1	raw egg yolk

1. Wash and dry the lettuce and tear into about 2-inch pieces. Add onions and cheese. Refrigerate.
2. Cube rye bread into ½-inch cubes and set on baking sheet in warm oven to dry into croutons.
3. To make dressing, mash garlic with 2 spoons in a dry bowl. Mash capers in the same bowl. Mash anchovy fillets in the same bowl.
4. Hammer whole peppercorns into a coarse powder and add to the above.
5. Add salt, adjusting to taste, Worcestershire sauce, mustard, lemon juice, olive oil, and vinegar.
6. Add raw egg yolk and mix all ingredients together. Chill dressing until ready to use.
7. Add croutons to salad just before adding the dressing.

Mysteriously, William Findlay's Caesar Salad recipe was garnered from "an Israeli sailor who was a cook" while Bill was with the TS on a trip to Ottawa. On the other hand, Bill's cello career has been clearly visible all the way — study at the famous Meadowmount Summer School in New York State and the Eastman School of Music, followed by becoming the youngest member of the TS in 1962 at the age of twenty-one. Among the many scholarships he has won, was one which sent him back to Eastman as a full-time student. He then rejoined the Symphony in 1969. In the last few years Bill has given solo performances with the Voirin Ensemble and the New Chamber Orchestra; he also teaches.

WILLIAM FINDLAY
Violoncello

Serves 4

1	large cucumber		3	spring onions or pearl onions, diced
	salt		½ cup	sour cream
2 tsp.	vinegar			paprika
1½ tsp.	sugar			

1. Peel cucumber and slice on single blade of grater. Slices should be very thin.
2. Salt lightly and let stand about 10 minutes.
3. Squeeze out the excess water.
4. In a salad bowl dissolve sugar in vinegar. Add cucumber, onion, and sour cream. More vinegar and sugar may be added if desired.
5. Serve sprinkled with paprika.

Serve with Chicken Paprikas and Dumplings (p. 48).

GEORGE HORVATH
Violoncello

Serves 4

½ cup   lean salt pork, cubed   ½   medium young red cabbage

1. Set oven to 450° F.
2. Render salt pork slowly in frypan.
3. Finely shred cabbage and place loosely in glass loaf dish.
4. When salt pork is crisp, pour dripping and salt residue and crisp, not burned, salt pork over cabbage.
5. Toss mixture and place in preheated oven until crisply cooked (about 10 minutes).

Serve on separate salad dishes as an appetizer with hot French bread or with Pork Pot Piquant (p. 74).

Bernard Temoin's French grandmother brought her red cabbage recipe with her when she came to Canada from a small town near Paris.

Bernard was born in Vancouver. He fell in love with the clarinet early, and played with the Kitsilano Boys' Band on its many European tours. A degree in piano from the Royal Conservatory and in clarinet from the Juilliard School of Music brought him full circle to the Vancouver Symphony, where he played under such giants as Beecham, Klemperer, and Barbirolli. 1950 saw him moving east and joining the wind section of the TS. Today, in addition, he teaches clarinet to the Toronto Symphony Youth Orchestra.

BERNARD TEMOIN
Clarinet

Serves 6 - 8

1 cup	whole wheat berries or kernels, cooked
2 cups	brown rice, cooked
1 ⅓ cups	grated Cheddar or Parmesan cheese
2 tsp.	salt
2	onions, coarsely chopped
4	stalks celery, chopped

Dressing:

⅓ cup	oil
1 Tblsp.	(or more) curry powder
3 Tblsp.	lemon juice
⅓ cup	cider vinegar
3 Tblsp.	honey
1 cup	raisins

1. Cook whole wheat berries and rice separately. While still hot, mix together. Add grated cheese and salt, and toss until cheese melts. Chill well.
2. To prepare dressing, heat the oil in a small saucepan. Add curry powder and sizzle it for one minute. Stir in remaining ingredients and simmer until raisins puff up (about 7 - 8 minutes).
3. To assemble salad, toss the grains gently to separate kernels; then toss in the chopped celery and onions. Pour dressing over the mixture and combine well. Chill until ready to serve.

AUDREY KING
Violoncello

Serves 6 as a salad

2 15-oz.	cans black-eyed peas (drained)		½ cup	thinly sliced onions
1 cup	salad oil		1 tsp.	salt
1¼ cups	wine vinegar			pepper to taste
1	clove garlic			

1. Mix all ingredients together and let stand in refrigerator for 24 hours.
2. Drain; remove garlic, and serve.

Principal flutist Jeanne Baxtresser came to The Toronto Symphony in 1978 after nine years in the same role with the Montreal Symphony Orchestra. Born in Bethlehem, Pennsylvania, Jeanne grew up in Minneapolis and studied at the Juilliard School of Music in New York. "My mother loves to entertain," she says, "and has been serving Texas Caviar for buffets for years."

JEANNE BAXTRESSER
Principal Flute

Serves 5 - 6   Middle Eastern Cracked Wheat Salad

½ lb.	cracked wheat		2½ Tblsp.	dried crushed mint or
3¾ Tblsp.	chopped onion			3¾ Tblsp. fresh mint, chopped
	salt and pepper		5 Tblsp.	olive oil
2 cups	finely chopped fresh parsley		5 Tblsp.	lemon juice
				cooked vine leaves, or raw lettuce
				or cabbage leaves (optional)

1. Soak cracked wheat in water to cover for 30 minutes. Drain and squeeze out as much moisture as possible with your hands. Spread on a cloth to dry further.
2. Mix in onion, squeezing with your hands to crush out the juice from the onions.
3. Season to taste with salt and pepper.
4. Add parsley, mint, olive oil, and lemon juice. Mix thoroughly.
5. Correct seasoning. The salad should have a distinct lemon flavour.
6. Serve in separate bowls lined with leaves, or in a large bowl to be scooped out with leaves.

   A little finely chopped tomato and/or cucumber may be added for colour. The cucumber must be salted and allowed to drain for 30 minutes so that water will not upset the balance of the various seasonings.

For contra bassoonist Bruce Bower, cooking is a relaxing hobby that goes along with entertaining because he likes to invite his friends to try out his culinary triumphs. One of these is his Tabbouleh. Less exotic, but very special, are his World's Greatest Bran Muffins (p. 170), which he says are exactly that.

BRUCE BOWER
Contra Bassoon

Serves 8 - 10

1	package cranberries	1 cup	sugar
1 16-oz.	can crushed pineapple	2	bananas, sliced
1 lb.	miniature marshmallows	¾ cup	whipping cream, whipped

1. Grind cranberries.
2. Add pineapple, marshmallows, and sugar, and mix well. Leave overnight in refrigerator.
3. Add bananas and whipped cream; fold.
4. Chill until ready to serve.

DONALD KUEHN
Principal Percussion

Serves 4 - 6

1	cooked chicken or leftover chicken
2 7-oz.	cans sweet corn
1 14-oz.	can pineapple chunks

Homemade Mayonnaise:

2	egg yolks
1 cup	salad oil
2 Tblsp.	lemon juice or vinegar
	pepper, salt, and curry powder

1. Remove meat from bones and cut into bite-size pieces, removing skin.
2. Drain sweet corn and pineapple.
3. To make mayonnaise, beat egg yolks and add oil very slowly, drop by drop, until mixture is thick. Add lemon juice.
4. Season with salt, pepper, and enough curry powder to give the mayonnaise some umph!
5. Combine chicken, sweet corn, and pineapple with mayonnaise to moisten ingredients thoroughly.

"My wife and I like this recipe on a hot summer day when we want to keep the cooking simple," says guest clarinetist James Campbell. "Homemade mayonnaise is essential. It's easy to make in the blender." Chicken à la Campbell can be dressed up for a festive buffet dish as well, he adds.

James Campbell's career as soloist since 1971 has spanned France, Germany, Yugoslavia, and Canada. He studied at the University of Toronto under Avrahm Galper, won first prize at the Canadian National Talent Festival and in the Jeunesses Musicales International Clarinet Competition in Belgrade, then studied for two more years in Paris. Since 1973 he has been a member of Camerata, a Toronto chamber music group.

JAMES CAMPBELL
Clarinet — Guest Artist

. . . *Sir Ernest MacMillan reigned as Music Director and Conductor for 25 years beginning in 1931, the longest tenure in the orchestra's history?*

. . . *that Sir Ernest, interned in Germany during World War I, was able to study music and work on the thesis that won him an Oxford doctorate while still a prisoner?*

. . . *that under MacMillan the TS began to expand in size, scope, and stature? Great names like Gigli, Chaliapin, Heifetz, Stravinsky, and Sir Thomas Beecham strode Massey Hall's stage.*

Yield: 6 dozen

1¾ cups	sifted flour		Frosting:	
½ tsp.	soda		2 cups	sifted icing sugar
½ tsp.	salt		5 Tblsp.	cocoa
½ cup	cocoa		½ tsp.	salt
½ cup	shortening or butter		3 Tblsp.	melted butter
1 cup	sugar		4 Tblsp.	milk
1	egg		1 tsp.	vanilla
½ cup	milk			
½ cup	pecans, chopped			
1 tsp.	vanilla			
36	marshmallows, cut in half			

1. Set oven to 350° F.
2. Sift flour with soda, salt, and cocoa.
3. Cream shortening; add sugar and cream thoroughly.
4. Add egg and beat well.
5. Add sifted dry ingredients alternately with the milk, starting and ending with the flour.
6. Add nuts and vanilla and stir to combine.
7. Drop by teaspoon on greased cookie sheet.
8. Bake for 8 minutes. Then top each cookie with a halved marshmallow and bake 2 minutes longer. Cool.
9. To prepare the frosting, sift the icing sugar with the cocoa. Add remaining ingredients and beat well.
10. Frost cooled cookies.

DONALD KUEHN
Principal Percussion

Yield: approximately 9 dozen

4 cups	self-raising flour or 4 cups all-purpose flour and 2 tsp. baking powder	2 tsp.	ginger
		⅔ cup	golden syrup, warmed
1 cup	margarine	1½ cups	brown sugar, firmly packed

1. Rub margarine into sifted flour.
2. Add ginger, warmed syrup, and sugar.
3. Mix well to a smooth dough.
4. Divide dough in half. Mould each half into two rolls approximately 12 inches long between sheets of waxed paper.
5. Refrigerate overnight.
6. Set oven to 350° F.
7. Slice dough into thin slices (¼ inch thick).
8. Bake for 8 minutes, or until lightly brown at edges, on lightly greased cookie sheets.

Noted for her flawless vocal technique and unexcelled interpretive ability, Dame Janet Baker is best known in North America as a recitalist and orchestral soloist, but she has also received great acclaim in Europe for her operatic roles. She was honoured by Her Majesty Queen Elizabeth with the title of Dame Commander of the Order of the British Empire in 1976.

Dame JANET BAKER
Mezzo-soprano — Guest Artist

Yield: 3 dozen

½ cup	butter		½ tsp.	baking powder
½ cup	brown sugar		½ tsp.	baking soda
½ cup	white sugar		½ tsp.	salt
1	egg		1 cup	rolled oats
1 tsp.	vanilla		¾ cup	semi-sweet chocolate chips
1 Tblsp.	milk		1 Tblsp.	grated orange rind
1 cup	flour			

1. Set oven to 350° F.
2. Cream butter and sugars together.
3. Add egg, vanilla, and milk.
4. Sift together flour, baking powder, baking soda, and salt, and add.
5. Add oats, chocolate chips, and orange rind, and mix.
6. Drop by spoonfuls onto lightly greased cookie sheet.
7. Flatten with fork dipped in hot water and bake 10 - 15 minutes.

DAVID AND JEAN WULKAN
Violins

Yield: 3 - 4 dozen

3 cups	flour	1½ cups	sugar
1 tsp.	salt	2	eggs
½ tsp.	baking powder	1 tsp.	vanilla
½ tsp.	baking soda	8 oz.	sour cream
½ cup	margarine		cinnamon sugar

1. Set oven to 400° F.
2. Combine the flour, salt, baking powder, and baking soda.
3. Cream the margarine and sugar; add eggs and vanilla and beat well.
4. Add flour mixture alternately with sour cream to butter mixture. Drop by tablespoon on greased cookie sheet.
5. Sprinkle with cinnamon sugar before putting into oven.
6. Bake about 12 minutes or until slightly browned.

STEPHANIE CHOMYK
Viola

Yield: 2½ - 3 dozen biscuits

1 lb.	butter	5 cups	pastry flour
1	egg yolk	pinch	baking powder
1 cup	fruit sugar (very fine, not icing)	pinch	baking soda

1. Set oven to 300° F.
2. Cream softened butter; add yolk and mix well.
3. Blend in sugar.
4. Gradually add sifted dry ingredients, eventually using your hands when it becomes too difficult to mix with spoon. Mixture should come away clean from bowl.
5. Taking about a quarter of the mixture at a time, roll out between two pieces of waxed paper to about ¼-inch thickness. (If too thin, shortbread will brown too much.)
6. Cut with favourite cookie cutter.
7. Place on ungreased sheet and prick each piece.
8. Bake 30 minutes.

Jan Whyte's Royal Shortbread recipe was given to her years ago by her children's English nanny who claimed it came from Buckingham Palace.

After studying at the Royal Conservatory of Music with Albert Pratz, Jan returned to her home in Vancouver and played in the Vancouver Symphony Orchestra for three years before joining the violin section of The Toronto Symphony in 1957. For many years she has been playing either in a string quartet or in a violin and cello duo in the Symphony school programs. She also teaches privately and coaches the violin and viola players in a school orchestra for the Toronto Board of Education.

JAN WHYTE
Violin

Serves 6 - 8

1 cup	cut-up dates		1¾ cups	flour
1 cup	boiling water		1 tsp.	baking soda
⅔ cup	shortening		2 Tblsp.	cocoa
1 cup	sugar		½ tsp.	salt
1 tsp.	vanilla		½ cup	chopped nuts
2	eggs			

Topping:

1 6-oz.	package of chocolate chips
2 Tblsp.	sugar
½ cup	chopped nuts

1. Set oven to 350° F. Grease a 9 x 13-inch pan.
2. Combine dates and water. Set aside.
3. Cream shortening and add sugar, vanilla, and eggs. Beat well at high speed.
4. Sift together flour, soda, cocoa, and salt. Add alternately with dates and water to creamed mixture.
5. Add nuts. Pour mixture into pan and sprinkle with topping.
6. Bake 40 to 50 minutes and cut into squares.

AUDREY KING
Violoncello

Dutch Butter Cake

½ lb. butter
½ lb. sugar (1 cup)

1 tsp. almond or lemon extract
½ lb. flour (2 cups)

1. Set oven to 400° F.
2. Cream together butter, sugar, and extract.
3. Add flour gradually.
4. Knead with hands into a soft dough.
5. Pat into ungreased 8 x 12-inch baking dish.
6. Bake 15 - 20 minutes. Cake is still soft and looks uncooked when taken from oven.
7. Allow to cool slightly. Cut into squares and remove from pan while still warm.

JACOB GROOB
Violin

Base:

1 cup	all-purpose flour	
¼ cup	sugar	
½ cup	cold butter	

Filling:

1 6-oz.	package dried apricots	⅓ cup	all-purpose flour
2	eggs	½ tsp.	baking powder
1 cup	less 1 Tblsp. brown sugar	¼ tsp.	salt
1 tsp.	vanilla		

1. Set oven to 350° F.
2. Sift flour and sugar together; cut in butter with pastry cutter. Pat down into an ungreased 9- or 10-inch square pan.
3. Bake 15 - 20 minutes or until golden. Cool.
4. Wash apricots, cut into slivers with scissors, and cook over low heat in enough water just to cover for 5 minutes, stirring constantly.
5. Drain well and cool.
6. Beat eggs lightly, adding sugar gradually. Beat until thick. Add vanilla.
7. Add sifted dry ingredients, mixing only until flour disappears. Fold in cooled apricots until well distributed. Pour onto cooled base and bake for 35 minutes or until done.
8. Pat down gently and cool.
9. Sprinkle with icing sugar and cut into squares.

JEAN AND DAVID WULKAN
Violins

¾ cup	butter	½ cup	lemon juice
½ cup	sifted confectioner's sugar	2	eggs, separated
1½ cups	flour	¼ cup	white sugar
½ cup	custard powder	⅓ cup	shredded coconut
1 cup	sweetened condensed milk		

1. Set oven to 350° F.
2. Cream butter and sugar. Work in flour and custard powder. Press into 9 x 11-inch oblong pan and bake for 15 minutes.
3. Mix milk, lemon juice, and egg yolks, and spread on top of cooked base.
4. Whip egg whites until stiff, beat in sugar, and fold in coconut.
5. Spread over the filling and bake for 15 minutes.
6. When cool, cut into squares or bars.

STEPHANIE CHOMYK
Viola

Yield: 2 loaves

⅞ cup	butter, margarine, or oil		1 tsp.	soda
2 cups	brown sugar		½ tsp.	cinnamon
4	eggs, beaten		½ tsp.	cloves
2 cups	raisins		½ tsp.	nutmeg
3 cups	raw apple, diced finely		¼ tsp.	salt
1 cup	cold water		1 cup	chopped walnuts
3 cups	all-purpose flour			

1. Set oven to 350° F.
2. Cream shortening and brown sugar until smooth and light.
3. Add beaten eggs and mix well.
4. Add the following, mixing after each addition: raisins, apples, cold water, sifted dry ingredients, and nuts.
5. Pour into well greased tube pan or 2 well greased loaf pans and bake at least 1 hour.

JACOB GROOB
Violin

Vienna Torte

Layers:

1 cup	butter
1½ cups	sugar
3	eggs
½ cup	milk
1 tsp.	almond extract
1 tsp.	vanilla
5 cups	flour
4 tsp.	baking powder

Filling:

2 cups	prunes
2 cups	water
1½ cups	sugar
1 tsp.	cardamom seed

Almond Icing:

¾ cup	unsalted butter
4 cups	icing sugar
¼ tsp.	salt
3 Tblsp.	milk
1 tsp.	almond extract

Cake:
1. Set oven to 350° F.
2. Cream butter and sugar. Add eggs, milk, and flavourings. Beat until smooth.
3. Add sifted dry ingredients and beat until smooth.
4. Divide dough into 5 or 6 parts. Roll out on a floured board to a thickness of ¼ inch. The torte should have at least 5 layers. The layers can be baked on cookie sheets, or on the bottom of layer cake pans. Layers can be rolled or patted.
5. Bake 15 - 20 minutes or until lightly browned. Cool.

Filling:
1. Boil prunes in 2 cups of water. Cool, drain, and stone.
2. Place prunes into a blender jar and add sugar and cardamom seed. Blend until smooth.
3. Place filling between layers of cake.

After defrosting, the cake may be decorated as follows: Using reserved icing, decorate the top of cake in shape of wheel with spokes. Between spokes place a small mound of prune purée. Top each mound with blanched almond or rosette of icing. Border inside of rim with quartered maraschino cherries. Chill.

Icing:
1. Beat butter with icing sugar until pale and light. Add salt, milk, and extract, and beat well.
2. Spread generously on sides and top of cold torte. Reserve 1½ cups for further decoration.
3. Put the torte in a tightly closed container and refrigerate or freeze for 3 days to a week. Freeze extra icing also.
4. Defrost before serving.

Nostalgic memories of Icelandic cooking bubble up in each of Winnipeger Pearl Palmason's contributions to this book. Even when her violin performances took her to London, New York, and Toronto, her mother's Vinaterta followed her each Christmas. Throughout her career with The Toronto Symphony, which began under the conductorship of Sir Ernest MacMillan, Pearl has paid tribute to her heritage with concerts and radio recitals in her ancestral Iceland.

PEARL PALMASON
Violin

	almonds, blanched and split	10 oz.	flour
5 oz.	butter	½ tsp.	baking powder
8 oz.	sugar	½ cup	milk
3	egg yolks	3	egg whites
½	lemon, juice and grated rind		

1. Set oven to 325° F.
2. Grease and flour a 1-quart charlotte mould. Decorate the bottom with split almonds.
3. Cream butter and sugar. Beat for 10 minutes.
4. Beat in egg yolks, one at a time, beating well after each addition. Add lemon juice and rind.
5. Sift together the flour and baking powder.
6. Gradually add the flour alternately with the milk.
7. Beat the egg whites until stiff. Fold lightly into the mixture.
8. Bake 1 hour, or until cake tester comes out clean.

Appropriately, composer Oskar Morawetz's cake recipe has a musical history. "I got it from a former chef of Toscanini's whom I met at Lake Placid. She said it was one of the maestro's favourites." Oskar Morawetz's compositions have been favourites with Canadian and international audiences since his arrival in Canada from Czechoslovakia in 1940. The University of Toronto music professor has since had his work performed by all major Canadian artists.

Dr. OSKAR MORAWETZ
Composer

Serves 10 - 12

		Filling:	
8	eggs, separated	1 15-oz.	can sweetened chestnut purée (Swiss preferred)
8 Tblsp.	sugar	1 pint	whipping cream
8 level Tblsp.	all-purpose flour		sugar to taste
½ tsp.	baking powder	2-3 Tblsp.	rum or ½ tsp. rum extract

1. Set oven to 325° F. Butter and flour a 9 x 13-inch pan or 2 round pans.
2. Beat egg whites until stiff. Store in refrigerator until ready to use.
3. Beat egg yolks and sugar until light and bubbly.
4. Sift flour with baking powder and add slowly by the tablespoon to the beaten egg yolk mixture.
5. Fold in egg whites and pour into pan.
6. Bake about 40 minutes. Test for doneness.
7. Cool. Slice the rectangular cake through middle into halves. If desired, cut each of these in half again with a very sharp knife, to make 4 layers.
8. To make the filling, mix chestnut purée in a bowl with 3 Tblsp. cream to make it smooth. Add sugar to taste and rum or flavouring.
9. Fill cake with this mixture, reserving a little for decoration.
10. Whip cream and spread on top and sides. Decorate with sieved purée. Chill well before serving.

GEORGE HORVATH
Violoncello

UKRAINIAN HONEY CAKE

1 cup	honey (prairie buckwheat preferred)		½ tsp.	salt
½ cup	butter		1 tsp.	cinnamon
1 cup	brown sugar, firmly packed		1 cup	sour cream
4	eggs, separated		½ cup	raisins (optional)
3 cups	all-purpose flour		½ cup	chopped walnuts (optional)
2 tsp.	baking soda			icing sugar (for decorating)
½ tsp.	baking powder			

1. Set oven to 325° F.
2. Bring honey to a boil and cool.
3. Cream butter and sugar. Beat in egg yolks one at a time.
4. Add honey and beat well.
5. Combine dry ingredients and add to batter alternately with sour cream.
6. Stir in raisins and nuts.
7. Stiffly beat egg whites and fold into mixture.
8. Pour mixture into 10-inch tube pan or bundt pan and bake for 1 hour.
9. Cool in pan for 20 minutes before inverting. When cool, sift icing sugar over top.

Violinist Vera Tarnowsky and horn player John Simonelli are yet another TS husband-and-wife team who relish food as well as music. Vera's Honey Cake reflects her Winnipeg-based Ukrainian background, while the Philadelphia Apple Cake (p.133) came from a colleague in the Philadelphia Orchestra.

Vera began violin lessons at the age of six. Today, chamber music takes up whatever time is available from Symphony responsibilities. John, a graduate of the Curtis Institute, first played with the TS from 1962 to 1965, left it for the Philadelphia Orchestra, then rejoined the Symphony in 1975. He also teaches and freelances.

VERA TARNOWKSY
Violin

Serves 6 - 8

1½ cups	oil
2 cups	brown sugar, loosely packed
3	eggs
3 cups	all-purpose flour (½ all-purpose and ½ whole wheat if preferred)
1 tsp.	salt

1 tsp.	cinnamon
1 tsp.	baking soda
1 tsp.	vanilla
3 cups	peeled and coarsely chopped apples
1 cup	walnuts, chopped
1 cup	raisins
½ cup	red candied cherries, halved (optional, but a colourful addition for festive times)

1. Set oven to 350° F.
2. Butter and flour a 9-inch angel food pan or fancy cake mould.
3. Beat oil and sugar together; then add eggs until creamy.
4. Sift together dry ingredients and add to batter with vanilla, fruits, and nuts.
5. Bake for 1 hour and 15 minutes.

This cake is delicious 'plain' and can also be served with ice cream. A Brown Sugar Glaze can be added if desired.

Brown Sugar Glaze:

½ cup	butter or margarine
¾ cup	brown sugar, firmly packed

¼ cup	milk or cream

1. Combine all ingredients and cook over medium heat until mixture boils. Stir constantly.
2. Boil for 3 minutes. Spread on cake while still warm.

VERA TARNOWSKY
Violin

1¼ cups	boiling water
1 cup	oatmeal
½ cup	butter
¾ cup	white sugar
1 cup	brown sugar
1 tsp.	vanilla
2	eggs
1⅓ cups	flour
1 tsp.	soda

½ tsp.	salt
¾ tsp.	cinnamon
¼ tsp.	nutmeg

Coconut Frosting:

¼ cup	melted butter
½ cup	brown sugar
6 Tblsp.	cream
¾ cup	chopped walnuts
1 cup	shredded coconut

1. Set oven to 350° F. Grease and flour a 9 x 9-inch pan.
2. Soak the oatmeal in boiling water, covered, for 20 minutes.
3. Beat butter and sugars together until pale and fluffy.
4. Add vanilla and eggs, beating well.
5. Add oatmeal, mixing well.
6. Sift together dry ingredients and blend into above mixture.
7. Pour into pan and bake for 50 to 60 minutes.
8. Make the frosting.
9. While cake is still hot, cover with frosting and broil until bubbly.

VERA TARNOWSKY
Violin

Serves 8   Norwegian Prince's Cake

2 cups	flour	¾ cup	icing sugar
2 Tblsp.	baking powder	1 tsp.	cinnamon
1	egg	1 tsp.	ground cardamom
½ cup	sugar	4	egg whites
½ cup	softened margarine	1 4-oz.	package ground almonds

1. Set oven to 275° F.
2. Lightly grease 9-inch cake tin.
3. Sift flour and baking powder.
4. Beat egg and sugar together.
5. Add the egg mixture to sifted flour with softened margarine. Work into a 'plastic' texture.
6. Mould two-thirds of the dough into the cake tin, making a thin mould. Reserve trimmings and remaining one-third of dough for pattern on top of cake.
7. Sift together the icing sugar, cinnamon, and cardamom.
8. Beat the egg whites until very stiff; fold in spiced sugar and ground almonds.
9. Pour into prepared cake tin. Decorate with ¼-inch strips of dough arranged in a criss-cross or other pattern.
10. Bake for 1 hour, or until golden and mixture is set.

Guest artist Hugh McLean's recipe is a favourite that his Norwegian wife used to bake frequently in response to a standing order from Hugh and his three sons.

Hugh McLean, organist and musicologist, is Dean of the Faculty of Music at the University of Western Ontario.

HUGH McLEAN
Organ — Guest Artist

Serves 6 - 8

Crust:

⅓ cup	sweet butter
1 Tblsp.	sugar
1	egg yolk
1½ cups	cake and pastry flour

Filling:

1 lb.	cream cheese
1 cup	sugar
2	egg yolks
2 Tblsp.	flour
1 cup	milk
½ cup	raisins (washed and dried)
½	lemon, juice and rind

1. Set oven to 350° F.
2. Mix together ingredients for crust and pat in bottom of springform pan.
3. Mix ingredients for filling in order given. Mixture will be rather liquid.
4. Pour into crust and bake for 1 - 1¼ hours.

JACOB GROOB
Violin

Serves 12

Crust:

35	graham crackers, finely rolled
½ cup	melted butter or margarine

Filling:

1 3-oz	package lemon jelly powder
1 cup	hot water

1 8-oz.	package softened cream cheese
1 cup	sugar
1 tsp.	vanilla or 1 Tblsp. lemon juice
1 13-oz.	can evaporated milk, chilled in freezer for 30 - 45 minutes

1. Set oven to 350° F. Grease 10 x 14-inch glass baking dish.
2. Combine melted butter and cracker crumbs for the crust. Mix well. Reserve 2 cups of crumbs and press the remainder into the bottom of the baking dish.
3. Bake crust for 10 minutes. Allow to cool before adding filling.
4. Dissolve jelly powder in the hot water and allow to set in the refrigerator until it is the consistency of raw egg white.
5. Cream softened cheese with sugar and flavouring. Add gelatin mixture.
6. Beat chilled evaporated milk until stiff; then fold into gelatin mixture.
7. Spread over cooled crust, and sprinkle remaining crumbs over the top. Chill overnight or until firm.

Barbara Bloomer enjoys cooking as a relaxation from the tension of playing the French horn, which is, she says, "a challenging and elusive instrument demanding increasing practising in order to keep in top form". She comes by her talent honestly: her father was also a French horn player, who taught at the Eastman School of Music and was a member of the Rochester Symphony Orchestra. An Eastman graduate herself, Barbara went to the Buffalo Symphony Orchestra before coming to the TS in 1966. Besides private teaching and coaching horn quartets, she teaches almost every day in five schools for the North York Board of Education. Every year in June, she takes off for Sweden for a month's private study with a "marvellous, world-famous horn player, Lanzky-Otto".

BARBARA BLOOMER
Horn

. . . *that during the Depression Massey Hall also played host to cooking schools and wrestling matches?*

. . . *in 1944 the City of Toronto made its first grant of $1,500 to the orchestra?*

. . . *the post-World War II period saw the Symphony offering radio pop concerts, concerts for children and students, and a new Wednesday night subscription series?*

. . . *Czech-born Walter Susskind was conductor of the Scottish National Orchestra and the Victoria Symphony in Melbourne before coming to the TS in 1956?*

. . . *Susskind introduced the works of such exotic composers (for that time) as Hindemith and Stravinsky to the orchestra's solidly classical repertoire?*

. . . *that Susskind founded the National Youth Orchestra and conducted its first concert in August, 1960?*

Serves 6

Pie Crust:

1½ cups	all-purpose flour
¾ tsp.	salt
½ cup	lard
2½-3 Tblsp.	water

Filling:

2 cups	milk
pinch	soda
1½ cups	brown sugar
pinch	salt and soda
4 Tblsp.	cornstarch
1 Tblsp.	butter
1 tsp.	vanilla
	whipped cream (for topping)
	chopped pecans (for decorating)

1. Set oven to 400° F.
2. Prepare pastry. Combine salt and flour. Add lard and blend with pastry blender or fingertips until it resembles coarse meal. Add water and mix gently with a fork.
3. Roll and place in pie plate. Bake until lightly brown, about 15 minutes. Cool.
4. To make the filling, scald milk but do not boil. Add pinch of soda.
5. Spread brown sugar in a thin layer in a frying pan over low heat. Stir frequently until sugar is noticeably darker.
6. Add pinch of salt and soda to sugar. Stir.
7. Add milk to sugar and stir well, dissolving any hardened lumps of sugar.
8. Make a paste with the cornstarch and enough cold water to make a thick liquid. Add to hot milk, stirring well over heat until thickened. Remove from heat and add butter and vanilla. Cool well.
9. Fill baked shell with filling and top with whipped cream. Decorate with chopped pecans.

Soprano Nancy Hermiston got off to an early start on two important aspects of her life — singing and cooking. At the age of three, she was trilling "Ain't She Sweet" with a family dance band in Warkworth, Ontario, while imbibing a taste for good food from her mother and grandmother, prize-winning cooks at the local county fair. Her Burnt Sugar Cream Pie is a home-cooked treat for those rare times between engagements with the Canadian Opera Company and other North American orchestras. Nancy's 1979 debut with The Toronto Symphony met with warm critical acclaim.

NANCY HERMISTON
Soprano — Guest Artist

Serves 6 - 8

1 9-inch	pie shell		1 tsp.	vanilla
¼ cup	butter		1 Tblsp.	rum or 2 tsp. brandy in which
1 cup	dark brown sugar, firmly packed			vanilla bean has been soaked for
3	eggs			a long time
⅜ cup	corn syrup		½ tsp.	salt
⅛ cup	dark molasses			
1½ cups	chopped pecans (⅓ of them very finely chopped)			

1. Set oven to 450º F.
2. Partially bake pie shell for 5 - 7 minutes. Cool.
3. Reduce oven temperature to 375º F.
4. Cream butter and sugar.
5. Beat in eggs, one at a time.
6. Mix corn syrup, molasses, pecans, vanilla, rum (or brandy), and salt, and stir into egg mixture.
7. Pour mixture into pie shell.
8. Decorate top with pecan halves.
9. Bake 45 minutes to 1 hour until knife inserted comes out clean.

SCOTT WILSON
Horn

Serves 6 - 8

	pastry for a 9-inch two-crust pie	¾ cup	sugar
3	eggs	¼ cup	flour
⅓ cup	butter, melted	¼ tsp.	salt
2 Tblsp.	lemon juice	1 20-oz.	can crushed pineapple, drained
½ cup	water		

1. Set oven to 400° F.
2. Have pastry ready.
3. Beat the eggs by hand and add the butter, lemon juice, and water. Blend at low speed.
4. Add the sugar, flour, and salt.
5. Beat until smooth and then stir in the pineapple.
6. Pour into the pastry shell and cover with a lattice top.
7. Bake for 35 - 40 minutes. Check after 15 minutes. If pastry is browning too quickly, lower the oven to 350° F. and bake longer.

VERA TARNOWSKY
Violin

Serves 6 - 8

Crust:

1¼ cups	graham cracker crumbs
¼ cup	granulated sugar
½ cup	melted or softened butter

Filling:

4	egg yolks
½ cup	granulated sugar
1	envelope of gelatin
¼ cup	warm water
2	egg whites
½ pint	whipping cream
¼ cup	rum
	semi-sweet chocolate (for decorating)

Crust:

1. Set oven to 375º F.
2. Thoroughly combine graham cracker crumbs, sugar, and butter.
3. Line 9-inch pie plate with foil and press crumb mixture against bottom and sides. Bake 8 minutes. Cool.

Filling:

1. Beat egg yolks with electric beater until light and fluffy. Add sugar slowly.
2. Soak gelatin in warm water and bring slowly to a boil. Let cool.
3. Beat egg whites until stiff. Beat whipping cream.
4. Add rum to yolk mixture.
5. Fold whipping cream and gelatin into egg mixture and, finally, fold egg whites into above mixture.
6. Pour mixture into graham cracker crumb shell and refrigerate overnight.
7. Shave semi-sweet chocolate (with potato peeler) over pie prior to serving.

"This a favourite dessert of many of our guest artists," says Walter Homburger of his rum-flavoured pie.

Managing Director of The Toronto Symphony since 1962, Walter Homburger guides the orchestra's multitudinous affairs with a hand on today and an eye for the future. "I live several years ahead," he says with a laugh, speaking of upcoming seasons. In addition to his position with the Symphony for which he has gained world-wide recognition and respect, he owns and manages his own company—International Artists Concert Agency—which he founded in 1947, six years after coming to Canada from Germany.

WALTER HOMBURGER
Managing Director of The Toronto Symphony

Serves 10

1	10-inch baked pie shell		juice of 1 lemon
2	mashed bananas	½ cup	whipping cream
1 16-oz.	can mashed pumpkin	2	packages gelatin
1½ cups	sugar	4	eggs, separated
1 tsp.	allspice		extra whipping cream (for serving)
1 tsp.	cinnamon		whole pecans (for decorating)
1 tsp.	cloves		

1. Add mashed bananas to pumpkin, sugar, spices, lemon juice in a large bowl.
2. Warm cream in top of double boiler and sprinkle gelatin over; allow to dissolve.
3. Add ingredients from step 1 and egg yolks. Cook until thickened. Cool.
4. Fold in beaten egg whites. Pour into baked pie shell and decorate with whipped cream and a few whole pecans.

Vanilla wafer crust may be used instead of pie shell. This delicious pie looks quite spectacular when served at the table. It takes a couple of hours to make because of the cooling time.

COROL McCARTNEY
Violin

Serves 6

Filling:

Crust:

1⅓ cups	graham wafer crumbs	3 4-oz.	packages cream cheese, room temperature
⅓ cup	brown sugar	2	eggs
⅓ cup	melted butter or margarine	1 tsp.	lemon juice
½ tsp.	cinnamon	1 tsp.	grated lemon rind
		¾ cup	white sugar
		1 tsp.	vanilla
		1 cup	sour cream

1. Set oven to 350° F.
2. Combine crumbs, brown sugar, cinnamon, and melted butter. Press into bottom and sides of a 9-inch pie pan.
3. Beat cream cheese, eggs, lemon juice and rind, sugar, and vanilla together until smooth and creamy.
4. Pour into the prepared crust and bake for 30 minutes.
5. Spread sour cream over the hot cooked pie and chill several hours before serving.

A Torontonian, viola player Kent Teeple joined The Toronto Symphony in 1977. "Completely Canadian-trained," he says of himself. Music fills his life, and he is an enthusiastic member of the chamber music ensemble called Accordes: A String Quintet, an unusual combination of instruments with a double bass instead of the customary second viola.

KENT TEEPLE
Viola

Serves 6

3	egg whites	⅔ cup	broken pecans
½ tsp.	baking powder	¼ tsp.	almond extract
1 cup	fruit or granulated sugar		whipping cream
14	crushed Ritz crackers		

1. Set oven to 350° F.
2. Beat egg whites until stiff but not dry.
3. Fold in baking powder, sugar, crushed Ritz crackers, pecans, and almond extract.
4. Pile into 8-inch buttered pie plate and bake 35 minutes.
5. Garnish with unsweetened whipped cream.

BERNARD TEMOIN
Clarinet

Pastry:

4 cups	flour
1¼ cups	shortening
1 tsp.	salt
8 Tblsp.	water

Filling:

1 cup	white sugar
1 Tblsp.	cinnamon
4 cups	chopped fresh mint leaves
2½-3 cups	plumped raisins (soak in hot water)

1. Set oven to 400° F.
2. Cut shortening and salt into flour and add enough water to hold together.
3. Roll out half of dough to cover 11 x 17-inch jelly roll pan (cookie tin with edges).
4. Mix sugar and cinnamon.
5. Chop fresh mint leaves (about size of a baby fingernail). Grandmother Barstow always washed and dried the mint, stripped the leaves off, put them in a drinking glass, and cut them with scissors.
6. Cover dough with raisins and mint.
7. Sprinkle with ¾ cup of sugar mixture.
8. Roll out top crust, cover, and crimp edge.
9. Prick with fork.
10. Spray top with a little water.
11. Sprinkle rest of sugar on top.
12. Bake in oven for 20 - 30 minutes or until pastry is done.
13. Cut into squares.

This recipe came from Northern England where it is a favourite of Chris' wife's family. You may use your own pastry recipe if you prefer.

CHRISTOPHER WEAIT
Co-Principal Bassoon

. . . the TS won warm praise from New York critics when it played for the first time at Carnegie Hall in the International Festival of Visiting Orchestras in December, 1963?

. . . that handling guest artists can be nerve-wracking? Artur Rubinstein would fine tune his appearances so closely that he would only arrive in town at 5:45 p.m. before a concert, play, and leave at midnight.

. . . Seiji Ozawa was senior assistant conductor of the New York Philharmonic under Leonard Bernstein when he first guest-conducted the TS in January, 1964?

. . . Ozawa, as the Symphony's new conductor, took the orchestra on its first tour of Britain for the Commonwealth Arts Festival in September, 1965?

. . . Ozawa introduced a series called "Jazz at the Symphony" as one of his innovations?

. . . Toronto audiences got their first taste of Japanese music played by Japanese musicians under Ozawa?

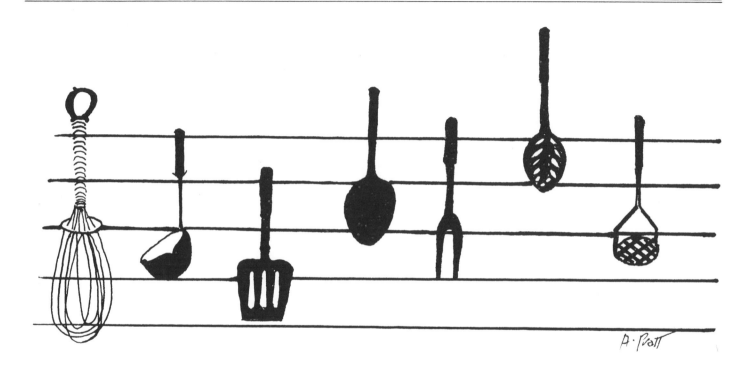

Serves 10 - 12

3	packages ladyfingers, or enough to line a springform pan (sides and bottom)
4	envelopes unflavoured gelatin
¾ cup	cold water
3 1-lb.	boxes frozen strawberries, thawed
⅛ tsp.	salt
3 cups	heavy cream, whipped

Glaze:

1 quart	fresh strawberries
¾ cup	sugar
1½ Tblsp.	cornstarch
¼ cup	cold water
	red food colouring

1. Butter lightly bottom and sides of 9-inch springform pan. Line sides and bottom with ladyfingers.
2. Soften gelatin in ¾ cup cold water; dissolve over low heat. Stir quickly into thawed strawberries and add salt.
3. In blender or food processor purée strawberry mixture. Fold cream into strawberry purée (in a large bowl). Pour contents into ladyfinger-lined springform pan.
4. Refrigerate several hours until mixture has stiffened. (Ideally, this should be made a day ahead and refrigerated overnight.) Add glaze a few hours before serving.

Glaze:
1. Crush enough uneven berries to make 1 cup. Keep the remainder whole.
2. Mix sugar, cornstarch, and ¼ cup cold water in saucepan. Add crushed berries, mix well, and cook, stirring until thickened. Cool. Add a few drops of red food colouring.
3. Arrange whole berries on cake and spoon glaze over fruit. Chill several hours. Remove to serving plate, leaving cake on pan base.

"It's a sweetheart of a dessert," says trombonist Murray Ginsberg fervently of his Strawberry Sonata. He applies the same exuberance to his musical reminiscences. "I first played with The Toronto Symphony on the third Saturday of January, 1938, at 1:30 p.m. at the age of fourteen." He followed this precocious start with a stint in the Canadian Army Show with Wayne and Shuster during World War II, appearances in the brass section of the Conservatory orchestra which led to joining the CBC Symphony at its inauguration, and a performance in the CBC's very first television show. Murray left the TS in 1979.

MURRAY GINSBERG
Trombone

Serves 24

1 cup	butter or margarine	⅓ cup	lemon juice
2 cups	sugar	7	eggs, separated
1½ tsp.	vanilla	1 cup	cream, whipped
1½ tsp.	grated lemon rind	1	large angel food cake

1. Thoroughly cream butter and sugar. Add vanilla, lemon rind, and juice. Mix well.
2. Add yolks, one at a time, mixing well after each addition.
3. Beat egg whites. Fold into lemon mixture and then fold in whipped cream.
4. Line a 13 x 9 x 2-inch baking pan with waxed paper (or use unlined Tupperware container).
5. Break angel food cake into small chunks and place alternately with filling in pan.
6. Cut through with spoon to fill all spaces.
7. Freeze immediately.
8. An hour before serving, remove to refrigerate.

This will keep in freezer for a couple of weeks.

SUSAN LIPCHAK
Assistant Principal Viola

Serves 8 — Make the day before serving.

1 package miniature marshmallows
1 cup boiling water
4 tsp. instant coffee
1 pint whipping cream

2 packages ladyfingers or chocolate
wafers
chocolate shavings and whipped
cream (for decoration)

1. In a double boiler combine the marshmallows, water, and coffee.
2. Stir constantly until marshmallows are melted. Place in refrigerator until firm — about 4 hours.
3. Whip the cream until it holds its shape. In another bowl whip the hardened marshmallow mixture.
4. Fold the two mixtures together.
5. Line 8- or 9-inch springform pan, sides and bottom, with chocolate wafers or ladyfingers.
6. Add half the mixture.
7. Add another layer of lady fingers or wafers.
8. Add other half of mixture.
9. Before serving, cover the top with shavings of chocolate and rosettes of whipped cream.

Victor Feldbrill's warm smile has been familiar to Toronto music-lovers for many years. A native Torontonian, he trained in his hometown in both violin and conducting. He has been associated with The Toronto Symphony in different capacities since 1949, presently serving as guest conductor. As well, he is conductor-in-residence at the Faculty of Music, University of Toronto, and musical director of the London Symphony. He has also conducted many orchestras around the world. He loves cooking — other people's — and one of his favourites is his wife's Mocha Cake.

VICTOR FELDBRILL
Guest Conductor

Serves 8 - 10

2 cups	graham wafer crumbs		8 oz.	cream cheese
½ cup	brown sugar		1 cup	icing sugar
⅓ cup	melted butter		1 19-oz.	can cherry pie filling (or strawberry
1	package Dream Whip			and rhubarb)

1. Combine crumbs, brown sugar, melted butter.
2. Press firmly into 9 x 12-inch glass baking pan.
3. Refrigerate.
4. Prepare Dream Whip according to directions on box.
5. Add softened cream cheese and icing sugar.
6. Whip until smooth.
7. Spread over crumb mixture.
8. Top with cherry pie filling.
9. Chill until ready to serve.

No wonder trumpeter, composer, and popular songwriter John Cowell spends little time on cooking. He began his career at fifteen as cornet soloist on CBC radio concerts, played solo trumpet with a Navy band during World War II, and joined The Toronto Symphony in 1952. En route, a scholarship in composition led to three years at the Royal Conservatory and the arranging and composing of symphonies, concertos, and solos for the trumpet — some of which were commissioned for the TS. His 125 popular songs have been recorded by top singers and orchestras, two reaching the top of the Hit Parade to become standards. Even with this activity, Johnny also manages to play with the Toronto Brass Society.

JOHN COWELL
Trumpet

Serves 4   **Manna from Heaven**

1½ cups	milk	⅙ cup	granulated sugar
¼ cup	wheatlets or Cream of Wheat	1 tsp.	vanilla
1	egg, separated	⅛ cup	ground nuts, preferably hazelnuts

1. Bring milk to a boil. Stir in cereal slowly and cook for about 5 minutes until thickened.
2. Beat egg yolk. Add sugar, vanilla, and nuts.
3. Gradually add lukewarm cereal mixture.
4. Beat egg white and fold gently into this mixture.
5. Chill.

Serve with a sauce of raspberries or strawberries, which should be a little juicy and not very sweet.

Young Canadian pianist Arthur Ozolins acquired his Latvian dessert recipe while living in Spain and studying in Paris — typical of his unusual life and career to date. Born in Germany of Latvian parents, Arthur grew up in Buenos Aires where he learned the piano from his mother and grandmother. After his mother's death, he came to Canada at the age of thirteen and studied at the Royal Conservatory. At fifteen he made the first of many appearances with The Toronto Symphony. Encouraged by Pablo Casals, he continued his studies and today is a figure on the international music scene.

ARTHUR OZOLINS
Piano — Guest Artist

Serves 8 - 10

1 cup	sugar	½ tsp.	salt
1 cup	water	¼ cup	shortening
½ tsp.	red food colouring (optional)	¾ cup	milk (approximately)
5 or more	medium apples, peeled and sliced	2 Tblsp.	melted butter or margarine
1½ cups	all-purpose sifted flour	2 Tblsp.	sugar
2 tsp.	baking powder	½ tsp.	cinnamon

1. Set oven to 450° F.
2. Mix sugar and water in a small pan, adding colouring, if desired. Bring to a boil and simmer for a few minutes.
3. Slice apples into greased 8 x 12-inch baking dish.
4. Pour syrup over apples.
5. Mix together flour, baking powder, and salt, and blend in shortening until mixture resembles the proverbial 'meal'.
6. Add enough milk to make a soft dough.
7. Drop twelve spoonfuls of dough on top of the apples, making a dent in the top of each mound.
8. Combine melted butter or margarine, sugar, and cinnamon, and place in the dents in the dough.
9. Bake for 25 - 30 minutes.

   Serve warm with cream or ice cream. It may also be served cold.

Now "a happy amateur", long time TS bass player Sam Levine left the Symphony in December '79 to become president of the Toronto Musicians' Association. Sam's more than thirty years with the orchestra date from the days of Sir Ernest MacMillan.

SAM LEVINE
Double Bass

Serves 6 - 8

Base:

1 cup	chocolate cookie crumbs
½ cup	finely chopped pecans
⅓ cup	melted butter

Filling:

8 oz.	milk chocolate
¼ cup	extra strong coffee
2	eggs, beaten
1 tsp.	vanilla
1 cup	whipping cream
2 oz.	semi-sweet chocolate, coarsely grated

Topping:

½ cup	whipping cream
2 Tblsp.	icing sugar
2 Tblsp.	cognac, coffee liqueur, or chocolate liqueur
1 oz.	semi-sweet chocolate for curls

1. Combine crumbs with nuts and mix with butter. Pat into a 9-inch springform pan. Refrigerate.
2. Melt chocolate in coffee in a double boiler.
3. Remove from heat; beat in eggs and add vanilla.
4. Beat cream until light (do not overbeat) and fold into the *cooled* chocolate with the grated chocolate.
5. Pour mixture into the springform pan and freeze until firm. This takes a few hours.
6. Whip remaining cream until firm and add sugar and liqueur. Beat until very stiff.
7. Pipe cream decoratively around the edges and in the centre and garnish with chocolate curls. Return to freezer.
8. Remove from freezer 10 minutes before serving.

This recipe, which Jean acquired during her Bonnie Stern cooking course, is a never-failing success.

JEAN WULKAN
Violin

Serves 8

1	egg white	2 Tblsp.	rum, tia maria, or amaretto
2 Tblsp.	sugar	¼ cup	toasted almonds, chopped
1 cup	whipping cream	½ cup	toasted flaked coconut
¼ cup	sugar	8	maraschino cherries
1 tsp.	vanilla		

1. Beat egg white until frothy. Add 2 Tblsp. sugar gradually, and continue beating until stiff.
2. Whip cream; add sugar and flavourings. Whip until stiff.
3. Mix almonds and coconut together and fold three-quarters of mixture into whipped cream.
4. Fold beaten egg white into whipped cream.
5. Spoon mixture into 8 small muffin soufflé cups or 8 paper cups set in muffin tins.
6. Sprinkle reserved nuts and coconut on top, and garnish each with a cherry. Freeze until firm.

Can be made into a pie by pouring mixture into a crumb crust or baked pie shell and freezing.

Jean acquired this recipe during her Bonnie Stern cooking course.

JEAN WULKAN
Violin

KARTOSCHKA

Potato

312 g	dry bread crumbs		100 g	vodka
250 mg	milk		120 g	butter (to taste)
200 g	sugar (white or brown)			cocoa

1. Combine all ingredients except cocoa.
2. Form in the shape of a potato.
3. Roll in cocoa to make it look dusty.

This a Russian dessert which is served on a plate in the centre of the table, then sliced, and eaten with the fingers.

Violinist Galina Bugaeva left an intensely busy musical life in Russia when she came to Toronto in 1974 and joined The Toronto Symphony. Born in Moscow, she studied at the Moscow Conservatory, then became a member of the Moscow Philharmonic. She also performed with the Bolshoi Symphony Orchestra of Radio and Television, was concertmaster of the orchestra of the Moscow Chamber Opera, and played chamber music. She says her recipe is typically Russian because of the vodka.

GALINA BUGAEVA
Violin

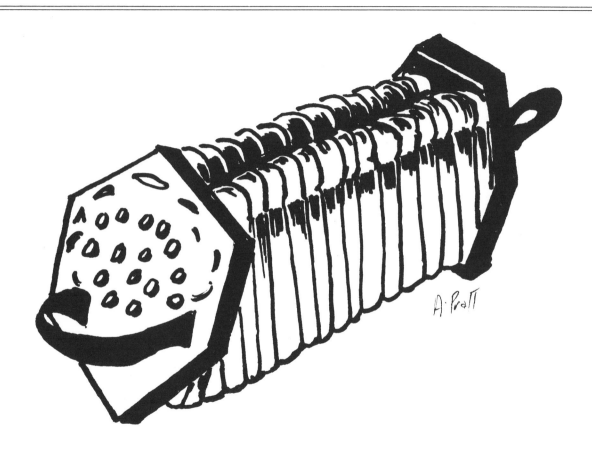

Yield: 2 5x9-inch loaves

2 cups	rolled oats (not instant)		2	yeast cakes dissolved in ½ cup
1 Tblsp.	salt			tepid water
2 Tblsp.	shortening		4½ cups	flour
2 cups	boiling water		2	beaten eggs (optional)
½ cup	dark molasses			soft butter

1. Mix first 5 ingredients and let stand until tepid.
2. Add yeast and flour, stirring well. Add eggs.
3. Brush top of dough with soft butter and cover tightly.
4. Let stand about 4 hours in moderately warm place.
5. Without kneading, put in greased bread pans and let stand until double in size.
6. Set oven to 375° F.
7. Bake 45 minutes.

In 1979 former Concertmaster Albert Pratz retired from The Toronto Symphony while celebrating a career of fifty years as a professional musician. He began with a broadcast on CFRB in 1919, and over the years was concertmaster with the Buffalo Philharmonic and the CBC Orchestra, and a member of the NBC Orchestra under Toscanini. His association with the TS began in the '30s. He himself studied with von Kunits and, today, some of his own pupils are with the orchestra. His wife's Oatmeal Bread recipe dates from World War I. It is light on the ingredients that were scarce in wartime.

ALBERT PRATZ
Former Concertmaster

Yield: 3 5x9-inch loaves

1	cake compressed yeast	2 cups	lukewarm water
1 Tblsp.	sugar	1½ tsp.	salt
½ cup	85° F. water	½ cup	sugar
1	egg, beaten	8 cups	all-purpose flour, sifted
½ cup	melted lard or shortening		

1. Have all ingredients at about 75° F.
2. Dissolve yeast and sugar in ½ cup water and let stand in warm place for 10 minutes.
3. Beat in egg, melted lard, water, salt, and sugar.
4. Add flour to liquid mixture a third at a time. Knead well.
5. Allow the bread to rise once in the bowl and once in the pan.
6. Place the loaves in a *cold* oven. Set heat to 400° F. After 15 minutes reduce heat to 375° F. and bake 25 minutes longer.
7. Remove loaves at once from pans and cool on a rack before storing.

"I'm a pretty basic cook," says TS guest artist, Mary Lou Fallis, "but this is my favourite bread recipe. It's such a boost for the ego because it never fails."

A Torontonian, Mary Lou studied voice with Maureen Forrester and Bernard Diamant. She spent a year in England with her husband, double bassist Peter Madgett, on a Canada Council grant. Today, she tours Canada constantly, filling singing engagements from the Yukon to Newfoundland.

MARY LOU FALLIS
Soprano — Guest Artist

Yield: 1 loaf

1	package active dry yeast	1 Tblsp.	dill seed
¼ cup	lukewarm water	1 tsp.	salt
1 Tblsp.	butter	¼ tsp.	baking soda
1 cup	cottage cheese	1 Tblsp.	sugar
1	egg, slightly beaten	2¼ cups	whole wheat flour
1	small onion grated		

1. Dissolve yeast in lukewarm water.
2. Melt butter in saucepan; add cottage cheese and heat until just warm.
3. In a large mixing bowl, combine and stir egg, onion, dill, salt, soda, and sugar.
4. Add yeast and cottage cheese mixture to the bowl and stir.
5. Gradually blend in the flour until the dough forms a sticky ball.
6. Cover bowl with a damp towel and place in a warm spot to rise for one hour.
7. With a wooden spoon punch dough down to its original size, then knead for a few minutes.
8. Place in a greased oven-proof glass loaf pan or 1½-quart casserole.
9. Again cover with towel and let rise for 35 minutes. Set oven to 350° F.
10. Remove towel; place loaf in oven and bake for 45 minutes. It may be necessary to lay a sheet of foil loosely on top for the last 15 minutes if the top begins to brown too much.
11. Cool in the pan for 30 minutes, then turn out on a wire rack for another 30 minutes before slicing.

DANIEL DOMB
Principal Violoncello

Yield: about 5 dozen

½	package dry yeast (1 tsp.)
3 cups	lukewarm water
½ cup	margarine, melted
1 cup	sugar
1 Tblsp.	salt
2	eggs
10-12 cups	flour

Variation: Whole Wheat Buns

4 cups	white flour
6 cups	whole wheat flour

1. Dissolve yeast in the lukewarm water.
2. Add melted margarine, sugar, and salt.
3. Add well beaten eggs.
4. Add flour gradually and mix well to a soft dough. Knead lightly.
5. Place dough in lightly greased bowl covered with damp cloth.
6. Mix this at 5:00 p.m.; knead down every hour until 10:00 p.m.
7. Shape into large walnut-size balls and place on lightly greased baking pans.
8. Cover with towel.
9. Let rise until morning.
10. Set oven to 350° F. and bake 15 to 20 minutes or until lightly browned.

These are delicious. Can be used for hamburgers, sandwiches, or just plain rolls.

SUSAN LIPCHAK
Assistant Principal Viola

Yield: 2 strudel-like coffee cakes

¼ cup	warm water
1 Tblsp.	sugar
1	package yeast
3 cups	sifted all-purpose flour
3 Tblsp.	sugar
½ tsp.	salt
½ cup	butter or margarine
½ cup	cold milk
2	egg yolks
½ cup	butter or margarine, softened

Filling:

1	19-oz.	can fruit pie filling or

Cheese Filling:

1	8-oz	package cream cheese
¼ cup		sugar
1		egg
dash		salt
½ tsp.		vanilla

1. Mix warm water, sugar, and yeast.
2. Sift together flour, sugar, and salt.
3. Cut in the ½ cup butter or margarine.
4. Add cold milk, egg yolks, and yeast mixture.
5. On a floured board roll dough to measure 12 x 18 inches.
6. Spread softened butter over two-thirds of dough.
7. Fold into thirds, cover, and refrigerate overnight or at least 2 hours.
8. On a floured board cut the dough in half and roll each half to measure 10 x 18 inches.
9. To make the cheese filling, beat together all the ingredients until smooth and creamy.
10. Spread filling down centre third of each piece of dough.
11. Slash sides of cakes in herringbone style, then crisscross strips over filling.
12. Allow to stand 30 - 45 minutes.
13. Set oven to 375° F.
14. Bake cakes on lightly greased cookie sheets for approximately 15 minutes.
15. Cool slightly and dribble over them a little glacé icing (sifted confectioner's sugar and a little water).

SUSAN LIPCHAK
Assistant Principal Viola

Yield: 1 9x13-inch cake

Bread Dough:

1 tsp.	sugar		⅛ tsp.	nutmeg
1¼ cups	tepid water		¼ tsp.	ground cloves
2 tsp.	dried yeast		¾ tsp.	cinnamon
1 tsp.	salt		½ cup	lard
3¾ cups	sifted flour		¾ cup	currants

Filling:

¾ cup	white sugar
⅛ tsp.	ginger

Glaze:

2 Tblsp.	sugar
2 Tblsp.	water

1. Dissolve sugar in water; sprinkle yeast over and let sit until bubbly, about 10 minutes.
2. Mix salt and flour; add yeast mixture to half of flour mixture.
3. Add rest of flour and knead thoroughly.
4. Let rise in warm place until double in size, about an hour.
5. Knead again until smooth.
6. To prepare the filling, blend all the ingredients except the lard and currants.
7. Roll out the dough on floured board to form a neat oblong.
8. Put half of the lard in small pieces over two-thirds of dough.
9. Sprinkle with half the currants and half the sugar and spice mixture.
10. Fold in three, bringing uncovered end of dough over first. Give half a turn and repeat from step 7.
11. Fold once more and roll out to fit a 9 x 13-inch pan.
12. Let rise 1 hour more and cut cross patterns on top with a sharp knife.
13. Set oven to 400° F. Bake until golden brown, at 400° F. for the first 20 minutes, then at 350° F. for an additional 25 minutes. Remove from pan and glaze at once.
14. To make glaze, blend together sugar and water and pour over cake.

This recipe has been a favourite of the Weait family for years. It came from Reading, England. Our branch of the Weaits only discovered it recently. It is wickedly rich and has a lovely crunchy top.

CHRISTOPHER WEAIT
Co-Principal Bassoon

Yield: 3 loaves

2 lb.	seedless raisins	3 tsp.	baking powder
1 lb.	brown sugar	1 tsp.	each cinnamon, nutmeg, and allspice
3 cups	lukewarm strong clear tea or	3	eggs
	3 cups Irish Whisky		melted butter or warm sweetened milk
1 lb.	all-purpose flour (4 cups)		(for glaze)

1. Soak raisins and brown sugar in tea or whisky.
2. Next day, set oven to 350° F. Grease three 8 x 4 x 3-inch loaf pans.
3. Sift together flour, baking powder, and spices.
4. Beat eggs.
5. Add flour mixture alternately with eggs to raisin mixture.
6. Turn into greased pans.
7. Bake 1½ hours or until cake tester comes out clean.
8. When cool, glaze with melted butter or warm sweetened milk. Return to oven for 5 minutes.

JEAN WULKAN
Violin

Yield: 2 loaves

2 cups	sugar		1 cup	salad oil
¼ tsp.	baking powder		3	eggs, slightly beaten
1 tsp.	cinnamon		1 tsp.	vanilla
3 cups	flour		2 cups	grated zucchini
1 tsp.	salt		1 cup	chopped walnuts
1 tsp.	soda			

1. Set oven to 325° F. Grease two loaf pans.
2. Sift together the dry ingredients.
3. Add oil, eggs, vanilla, zucchini, and nuts, and mix until blended.
4. Pour into loaf pans.
5. Bake for 60 - 75 minutes, or until done.

BARBARA BLOOMER
Horn

Serves 6 - 8

¾ cup	cornmeal	¾ tsp.	salt
1 cup	all-purpose flour	1 cup	milk
⅓ cup	sugar (I add a little more to make the bread a little sweeter)	1	egg, well beaten
3 tsp.	baking powder	2 Tblsp.	shortening (butter, chicken fat or beef dripping), melted

1. Set oven to 425° F. Grease an 8 x 8-inch shallow pan.
2. Sift together dry ingredients.
3. Mix milk, egg, and shortening, and add to dry ingredients. Mix lightly.
4. Bake 20 minutes.

This is easy, quick, and very nice for a snowy winter's Sunday Brunch. It is great with jelly and kids love it.

MARILYN MEYER
Viola

Yield: 12 muffins

1 cup	flour	⅓ cup	oil
2½ tsp.	baking powder	3	bananas, mashed
¼ tsp.	baking soda	½ tsp.	salt
¾ cup	bran	¾ cup	sugar
¼ cup	wheat germ		grape jelly
2	eggs		

1. Set oven to 400° F. Butter and flour muffin tins or use paper cups.
2. Sift together flour, baking powder, and soda into a large bowl.
3. Add bran and wheat germ and mix well.
4. Blend together eggs, oil, bananas, salt, and sugar.
5. Mix liquid with dry ingredients until just mixed.
6. Pour into prepared tins and place 1 tsp. grape jelly on top of each muffin.
7. Bake for 15 minutes.

COROL McCARTNEY
Violin

Yield: 1 dozen

1 cup	bran
1 cup	buttermilk
1 cup	flour
1 tsp.	cinnamon
1 tsp.	baking powder
½ tsp.	baking soda
½ tsp.	salt
⅓ cup	butter, room temperature

½ cup	brown sugar, packed
1	large egg
¼ cup	molasses
⅓ cup	raisins
⅓ cup	chopped dates or dried currants

Glaze:

¾ cup	honey
⅓ cup	corn syrup
1 Tblsp.	butter

1. Set oven to 400° F. Line muffin tins with paper baking cups or grease lightly.
2. Combine bran and buttermilk in large mixing bowl.
3. Into another bowl sift together flour, cinnamon, baking powder, baking soda, and salt.
4. Add to bran mixture, mixing until just moistened.
5. Cream together the butter, sugar, egg, and molasses. Blend into bran mixture. Add the dried fruit.
6. Divide among prepared muffin cups. Bake 20 - 25 minutes; cool slightly and remove papers. When cool, glaze.
7. To make the glaze, combine the ingredients in a small saucepan. Bring to boil over medium heat; reduce heat and simmer for 5 minutes.
8. Using a pair of spoons, dip muffins one at a time into glaze, coating thoroughly.
9. Place on cookie sheet or waxed paper and leave until glaze is set.

BRUCE BOWER
Contra Bassoon

Yield: 1½ dozen

1 cup	brown sugar		2 cups	flour, divided in two
½ tsp.	nutmeg		1 cup	raisins
½ tsp.	cloves		1 cup	sour cream
½ tsp.	cinnamon		1 tsp.	baking soda
½ cup	melted butter			

1. Set oven to 375° F.
2. Mix sugar and spices; add melted butter.
3. In another bowl mix 1 cup flour with raisins and add to sugar and butter.
4. Mix 1 cup flour with sour cream and soda.
5. Lightly mix all ingredients together.
6. Place in buttered muffin tins or paper cases.
7. Bake 30 minutes or until firm to the touch.

"My mother must have made a million of these when we were growing up, and we still love them," says clarinetist John Fetherston of his Spice Buns. John's father was Doug Fetherston, a violinist who was also with the TS at one time and, interestingly, for a few years, father and son performed together.

JOHN FETHERSTON
Clarinet

. . . three world-renowned conductors made their first TS appearance in the 1967/68 season? They were Colin Davis, Paul Kletzki, and Rafael Kubelik.

. . . the TS made its first far Eastern tour in 1969 with a triumphant visit to Japan?

. . . on its international tours the Symphony takes nearly 18,000 pounds of musical instruments?

. . . Karel Ancerl, Music Director of the TS from 1969 to 1974, and Herbert von Karajan, conductor of the Berlin Philharmonic, were born in the same week in 1908, and only 100 miles apart: Ancerl in Bohemia, and von Karajan in Salzburg?

. . . it was the summer of 1971 when the TS moved out under the stars and began to play at Ontario Place, and since then they've been rained out only once?

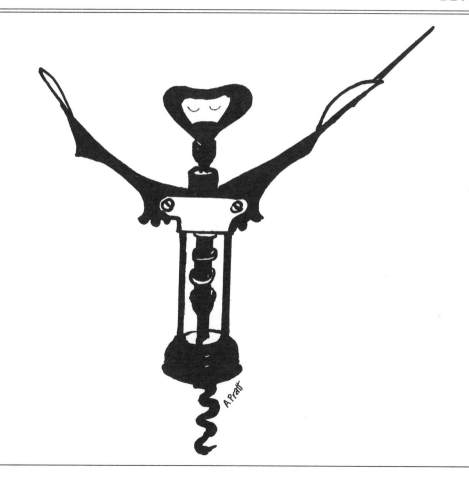

Serves 16 - 18

1 quart	fresh strawberries		1	bottle claret, chilled
½ cup	fine white sugar		2	bottles champagne, chilled
2	bottles dry white wine, chilled			

1. Combine the ingredients.
2. Top each serving with a strawberry.

Mrs. Aglaia von Kunits Edwards, daughter of the Symphony's first conductor, has contributed a cherished recipe and some equally cherished memories of the past.

"In 1911, my father, Luigi von Kunits, was widely acclaimed by his native Vienna. Outstanding musicians and friends came to hear him play his beloved Strad, and remained to pay homage. They were always invited back to our home and royally entertained. I often gaze at the large porcelain bowl now in my daughter's home, and wonder if it misses being filled to the brim with champagne, as in the good old days. Many well-known artists used to gather around this Royal Doulton bowl. Later on the rooms would resound with music. Quartets and solos were played until dawn."

AGLAIA von KUNITS EDWARDS

Serves approximately 8

1 cup	water
3	whole cardamom seeds
8	whole cloves
1	stick cinnamon
1	4-inch strip orange rind (orange part only)

¼ cup	whole blanched almonds
½ cup	seedless raisins
1	bottle bordeaux wine
1	bottle port wine
1¾ cups	vodka
	sugar

1. Bring water to a boil; then add cardamom seeds, cloves, cinnamon, and orange rind, tied in a cheesecloth bag.
2. Cover and simmer for about 10 minutes.
3. Add almonds and raisins and simmer 20 minutes. It may be necessary to add more water to cover fruit.
4. Add bordeaux, port, and vodka. Bring almost to the boil and remove from heat immediately.
5. Cool and refrigerate covered overnight or longer.
6. When ready to serve, remove spice bag and heat. Add sugar to taste.
7. Serve in heated punch glasses or mugs with a few almonds and raisins in each.

   I serve this around Christmas time. It is very potent but also very warming.

AUDREY KING
Violoncello

Yield: 4 - 4½ gallons

15 lb.	white sugar		¼ pint	ale yeast
3 gallons	soft water		1 lb.	sugar cubes
4 dozen	oranges		1 25-oz.	bottle white wine (sweet or dry)
10	lemons			

1. Dissolve 15 lb. sugar in water and bring to temperature of 120° F. Do not allow to boil. Keep skimming off the froth since the liquid must be clear.
2. Crush the juice from the fruit, retaining the orange skins.
3. Add the juice to the sugar and water.
4. Cool to room temperature.
5. Add yeast.
6. Allow to ferment for 48 hours.
7. During the 48-hour period rub sugar cubes over orange skins to remove zest. Add to the fermenting liquid.
8. Allow to ferment a further 48 hours in a large glass container. Do not use aluminum.
9. Strain into demijohn. Add wine.
10. Ferment for 6 to 8 months. When fermentation has stopped, strain into bottles using a Melitta filter paper.
11. Allow to age for approximately 1 year, testing frequently during that period.

Harry Freedman does not cook, but he does enjoy making wine and he has contributed the recipe of his favourite, which has been aged for fourteen years and has stood the test of time.

For almost twenty-four years, Harry played the English horn in The Toronto Symphony, retiring in 1970 so that he could devote more time to composing. His compositions have frequently been played by the TS.

HARRY FREEDMAN
Composer

Yield: 5 gallons   A Blend of California Grapes and Ontario Hybrids

Every fall hundreds of carloads of California grapes are imported into Ontario for the home winemaking market. Some of the more popular varieties are: Muscat, Alicante, Zinfandel, Carignano, and Grenache. These grapes usually come from the hot central valley of California. They are usually high in sugar and low in acid. They make a potent wine, with an alcohol content of thirteen per cent or higher. The Ontario hybrid grapes, on the other hand, are usually deficient in sugar and high in acid. A blend of the two will give you a well balanced wine.

The Ontario Hybrids are not as readily available as the California grapes. You may have to go to the Niagara area to find them.

1 bushel DeChaunac (5-9545)	1 package wine yeast
36 lb. (1 case) Grenache	

1. Crush grapes in an open container.
2. Add wine yeast.
3. Allow mash to ferment from 3 - 5 days. The mash is inclined to push up during fermentation and form a dry crust. Push it down once or twice a day to keep it wet.
4. Strain the must into a clean container and press mash to remove juice.
5. Allow fermentation to continue until it is very slow.
6. Syphon liquid into a carboy or gallon jugs and attach fermentation locks.
7. Rack when fermentation has stopped.
8. Rack again when wine is clear.
9. Age for 1 year.

ANTHONY ANTONACCI
Flute

Yield: Approximately 1 gallon

3 lb.	rhubarb	1 gallon (160 oz.)	water
2½ lb.	sugar	¼ tsp.	grape tannin
1½ tsp.	acid blend (or juice of 1½ lemons)		wine yeast
1 tsp.	yeast nutrient		

1. Cut up rhubarb into a clean plastic garbage can.
2. Pour sugar over rhubarb and leave for 24 hours.
3. Add remaining ingredients and allow to ferment for 48 hours.
4. Remove rhubarb from must, squeezing out as much juice as you can.
5. Skim must daily, allowing fermentation to continue until very slow.
6. Syphon liquid into glass carboy.
7. Attach fermentation lock or plastic wrap held in place with an elastic band.
8. Rack in about 1 month.
9. Rack again when wine is clear.

This wine is at its best when allowed to age for about 1 year.

ANTHONY ANTONACCI
Flute

Yield: 5 gallons

12 lb.	choke cherries	4 gallon	carboy of homemade beer
8 lb.	sugar		(before bottling)

1. Place cherries in plastic freezer bags and pour sugar over them. Tie up plastic bags and store in freezer until beer is ready.
2. After making beer, thaw cherries and sugar and place in a clean plastic garbage can.
3. Pour beer over cherries and leave for about 5 days.
4. Remove choke cherries and allow fermentation to continue until it slows to a gentle simmer.
5. Syphon into a glass carboy or gallon jugs and place air locks on them.
6. When fermentation has stopped, rack into clean containers.
7. Rack again when wine is clear.
8. Allow to age for at least 6 months.

This was inspired by an old English drink called Cherry Ale, using morello cherries, sugar, and old beer.

Anthony Antonacci's interests go far beyond the flute section of The Toronto Symphony. He teaches and he likes dabbling in the kitchen where he frequently cooks, but what he especially enjoys is winemaking. From the age of fifteen, he has been making wine, gallons and gallons of it. The preceding recipes are among his secrets.

A graduate of the Royal Conservatory, Anthony was at one time principal flutist of both the Canadian Opera Company orchestra and the National Ballet orchestra. He began his career with the TS in 1953.

ANTHONY ANTONACCI
Flute

. . . the Symphony's 1974 European tour included London, Vienna, and Bonn? In Vienna, two concerts at the famous Musikhalle were acclaimed by the discerning Viennese critics and audience.

. . . that once, during a Toronto Symphony tour, a suitcase containing all the scores for that evening's performance — Mahler's Fifth — disappeared only two hours before the concert was to begin? The solution? Another previously rehearsed work was quickly substituted and the concert went ahead on schedule.

. . . Maestro Andrew Davis studied and played the organ and harpsichord before becoming a conductor?

. . . prior to becoming Music Director and Conductor of the TS in 1975, Andrew Davis was assistant conductor of the BBC Scottish Symphony and the Philharmonia Orchestra?

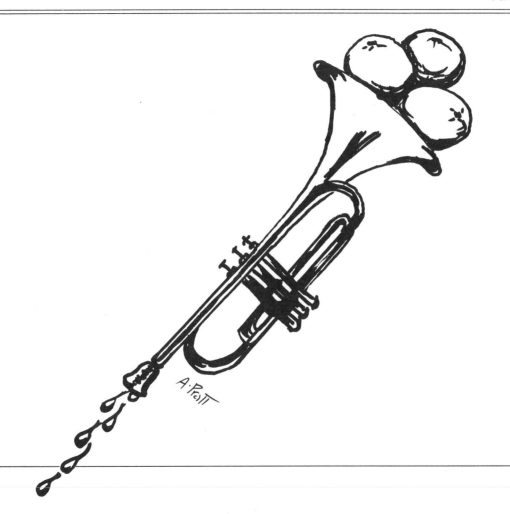

Yield: 1 quart

Make a special request to your favourite produce store as the cucumbers must be absolutely fresh. Any brown spots on the garlic must be cut away. Use zinc top jars with a rubber gasket. It is not necessary to sterilize the jars because of the salt present in the pickling brine.

	pickling cucumbers to fill a quart jar		several whole large stalks, stems
1 Tblsp.	coarse salt		included, of fresh dill (you cannot
¼ cup	hot water		put in too much dill)
1 Tblsp.	packaged pickling spices	1	hot pepper (optional)
4	cloves garlic		

1. In a small container dissolve salt in hot water.
2. Pack thoroughly scrubbed pickles in the clean jar with garlic and dill dispersed throughout.
3. Add dissolved salt, pickling spices, and pepper.
4. Fill the jar to the top with cold water; seal the jar tightly.
5. Store in a cool dark place.

   Two to three weeks will produce a moderately sour pickle; if you prefer, allow to mature for a longer period. Refrigeration will stop the pickling process. It is natural for the brine to become cloudy.

NORA SHULMAN
Associate Principal Flute

Serves 10 - 12

½ cup	milk	½ cup	vinegar
½ cup	white sugar	½ cup	butter
¼ cup	dry mustard	3	egg yolks

1. Blend all ingredients together until smooth.
2. Cook over hot water, stirring constantly until thickened.

Serve hot or cold.

This treasured recipe has been handed down for four generations.

NICHOLAS KILBURN
Co-Principal Bassoon

Serves 4 for breakfast

1	large egg, beaten		1	carton fruit yogurt,
1 cup	pre-sifted flour			any flavour (with honey)
2 tsp.	baking powder		1 Tblsp.	oil
			¼ tsp.	grated lemon or orange rind

1. Mix and stir all ingredients.
2. If batter seems thick, add milk in very small amounts until it is of a thick dropping consistency.
3. Drop on hot skillet from a cup or spoon to get 4-inch round cakes.
4. As soon as pancakes are puffed, bubbly, and golden brown on the underside, turn and brown the other side equally.

GUSTAV CIAMAGA
Dean of the Faculty of Music, University of Toronto

6 quarts	popped popcorn (1 cup unpopped)		2 tsp.	salt
4 cups	brown sugar		1 cup	corn syrup
1 lb.	butter		2 tsp.	baking soda

1. Set oven to 200° F.
2. Combine brown sugar, butter, salt, and corn syrup. Bring to a boil and boil for 5 minutes.
3. Remove from heat and add baking soda. This will cause mixture to "foam up like crazy, so be careful".
4. Pour sugar mixture over popcorn and mix well.
5. Spread on cookie sheets and bake for 1 hour.

Violinist Leslie Knowles says her Candied Popcorn recipe comes from her sister-in-law in a small Ohio town. "It's a farm recipe from Middle America," she laughs.

Born in Los Angeles, Leslie studied in Baltimore and New York and played with the Baltimore Symphony before joining the TS in 1976.

LESLIE KNOWLES
Violin

3-4 Tblsp.	peanut (or other) oil		fresh ground sea salt (or rock
½ cup	(approximately) popping corn		or regular salt)
2 Tblsp.	butter	1	bottle beer, chilled
½ cup	grated Cheddar cheese		

1. Heat oil in 2-quart saucepan over medium heat until quite hot. (One or two kernels popping corn may be added with oil; they will pop when it is ready.)
2. Add popping corn and cover.
3. Shake when kernels start to pop and continue until popping is completed.
4. Remove to large serving bowl.
5. Lower heat and melt the butter.
6. Add grated cheese to butter and allow to melt.
7. Sprinkle salt over popcorn to taste. Then pour melted butter and cheese mixture over popcorn, distributing evenly, and toss.
8. Open bottle of beer and consume with popcorn.

Bassoonist Mitchell Clarke, a one-time composer/arranger in the jingle business, says Transylvanian Popcorn "is good for after-concert snacks or when the midnight skulkers get the munchies."

Mitch studied bassoon with the Symphony's Nicholas Kilburn after graduation with a Bachelor of Music degree from the University of Toronto. In his free time he limbers up with squash and skiing, plays in Prelude Concerts for young children, and makes chamber music with the Toronto Concert Winds.

MITCHELL CLARKE
Bassoon

Chocolate Coating:

2	egg whites	
1 cup	sugar	
¼ cup	water	
½ lb.	walnuts, ground	

2 Tblsp.	butter
2 oz.	unsweetened chocolate
1 cup	icing sugar
3 Tblsp.	hot milk
	almond slices

1. Beat egg whites until stiff.
2. Boil sugar and water for 2 minutes.
3. Allow syrup to cool just a little. Pour into egg whites and stir.
4. Fold in ground walnuts and leave overnight in refrigerator.
5. Next day, set oven to 350° F.
6. Place teaspoonfuls of this mixture on a cookie sheet lined with foil and bake for 10 - 12 minutes (no longer as bottoms will burn). Cool on rack.
7. To make coating, melt butter and chocolate over hot water.
8. Add sugar and gradually stir in hot milk.
9. Take each candy and dip into coating. Press an almond slice into chocolate and let set.

A Torontonian, violist Harry Skura graduated from the Faculty of Music, University of Toronto. A stint with the Hamilton Philharmonic Orchestra was followed by a year of post-graduate studies at the University of Indiana with the famous violist, William Primrose. After a year with the National Ballet orchestra, Harry joined The Toronto Symphony in 1975. He is busy with numerous chamber music groups — string trios, string quartets, and piano quartets — and has played in the Symphony music education program, Prelude Concerts, for several years.

HARRY SKURA
Viola

. . . the Symphony carried out a memorable tour of China in 1977? Maureen Forrester and young pianist Louis Lortie were the soloists.

. . . during this tour, the ever alert Chinese noted Andrew Davis' birthdate in his passport and paraded a surprise birthday cake into his hotel dining room on that day?

. . . the peripatetic TS toured Western Canada and the American West Coast in April/May, 1979 and toured the American Midwest in the autumn of 1980, in addition to its annual appearances in Carnegie Hall?

. . . the TS under Maestro Davis, and with financial assistance from the Women's Committee, has recorded works by Borodin, Janacek, Tchaikowsky, and Respighi for CBS Records?

. . . the Borodin recordings won a Juno Award for best classical album of the year in 1978?

. . . Respighi's "La Boutique Fantasque", released in autumn, 1980 on CBS records, was the first work to be recorded by The Toronto Symphony in the new digital recording process?

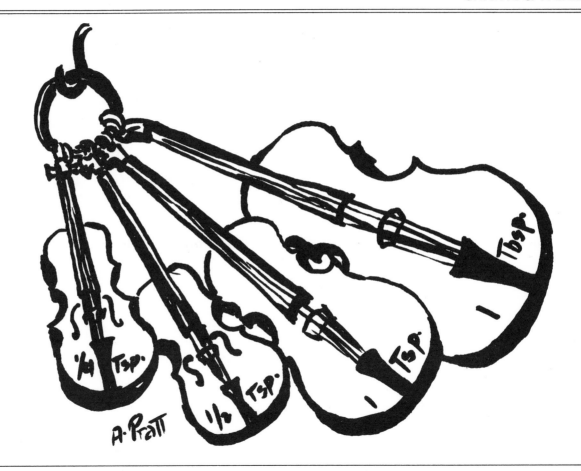

Liquid Measure	Actual		Convenient		
1 tsp.	5	mL	5	mL	
1 Tblsp.	15	mL	15	mL	
1 cup	237	mL	250	mL	
½ cup	118.5	mL	125	mL	
⅓ cup	79	mL	75	mL	
4 cups (32 oz.)	946	mL	1000	mL	(1 Litre)
1 pint (20 oz.)	568	mL	500	mL	
1 quart (40 oz.)	1137	mL (1.14L)	1250	mL	

To convert:

ounces to millilitres:	*multiply oz. x 29.57*
millilitres to ounces:	*multiply mL x 0.034*
litres to quarts (40 oz.):	*multiply litres x .88*
quarts to litres:	*multiply quarts x 1.14*

Weight	Actual		Convenient	
1 lb.	454	g	450	g
1 oz.	28.3	g	25	g
2.2 lb.	1	kg		

To convert:

grams to ounces:	*multiply g x 0.035*

Butter	2	cups	Raisins	3	cups
Dates	2½	cups	Sugar: brown, packed	2¼	cups
Flour: all-purpose	4	cups	confectioner's	3½	cups
cake	4½	cups	granulated	2	cups
whole wheat	3¾	cups	Walnuts	3½	cups
Peanuts, halved or chopped	3	cups			

2 Tblsp. flour	1 Tblsp. cornstarch, potato starch, rice starch
1 cup all-purpose flour	1 ⅛ cups cake and pastry flour
1 cup corn syrup	1 cup sugar and an additional ¼ cup of liquid used in the recipe
1 square of chocolate	3 Tblsp. cocoa and 1 Tblsp. fat
1 cup honey	1¼ cups sugar and 4 Tblsp. liquid
1 cup butter	1 cup margarine; 1 cup shortening and pinch of salt; 1 cup lard and pinch of salt. Melted fat equals solid measurement of fat.
1 cup table cream (18%)	⅞ cup milk and 3 Tblsp. butter
1 cup skim milk	3 Tblsp. skim milk powder and 1 cup water
1 cup buttermilk or sour milk	1 Tblsp. vinegar or lemon juice and enough milk to make 1 cup (let stand 5 minutes)
1 tsp. baking powder	¼ tsp. baking soda and ½ tsp. cream of tartar
1 whole egg	2 egg yolks
1 cup granulated sugar	1 ⅓ cups firmly packed brown sugar
1 clove garlic	½ tsp. instant minced garlic or garlic powder
2 Tblsp. green pepper	1 Tblsp. green pepper flakes
1 tsp. grated lemon rind	½ tsp. dried lemon peel
1 tsp. grated orange rind	½ tsp. dried orange peel
1 small onion	1 Tblsp. instant minced onion or onion flakes; 1 tsp. onion powder
1 Tblsp. snipped or chopped parsley	1 tsp. dried parsley flakes
1 package dry yeast	1 Tblsp. dry or 1 cake compressed yeast

THE TORONTO SYMPHONY COOKBOOK
215 Victoria Street
Toronto, Ontario. M5B 1V1

*A fund raising project of the Toronto
Symphony Women's Committee*

Please send me . . . . copies of *The Toronto Symphony
Cookbook* at $8.95 each, plus $1.00 per book to cover
mailing costs.

Enclosed is my cheque or money order for $ . . . .
made out to *The Toronto Symphony Cookbook,*
or CHARGEX . . . . / . . . . . . / . . . . . . / . . . . . .

Name . . . .

Street . . . .

City . . . . Province . . . .

Postal Code . . . .

*All proceeds from the sale of these cookbooks are for
the benefit of The Toronto Symphony.*

THE TORONTO SYMPHONY COOKBOOK
215 Victoria Street
Toronto, Ontario. M5B 1V1

*A fund raising project of the Toronto
Symphony Women's Committee*

Please send me . . . . copies of *The Toronto Symphony
Cookbook* at $8.95 each, plus $1.00 per book to cover
mailing costs.

Enclosed is my cheque or money order for $ . . . .
made out to *The Toronto Symphony Cookbook,*
or CHARGEX . . . . / . . . . . . / . . . . . . / . . . . . .

Name . . . .

Street . . . .

City . . . . Province . . . .

Postal Code . . . .

*All proceeds from the sale of these cookbooks are for
the benefit of The Toronto Symphony.*

THE TORONTO SYMPHONY COOKBOOK
215 Victoria Street
Toronto, Ontario. M5B 1V1

A fund raising project of the Toronto Symphony Women's Committee

Please send me .... copies of *The Toronto Symphony Cookbook* at $8.95 each, plus $1.00 per book to cover mailing costs.

Enclosed is my cheque or money order for $ . . . . made out to *The Toronto Symphony Cookbook,* or CHARGEX . . . . / . . . . . . / . . . . . . / . . . . . .

Name . . . .

Street . . . .

City . . . . Province . . . .

Postal Code . . . .

All proceeds from the sale of these cookbooks are for the benefit of The Toronto Symphony.

THE TORONTO SYMPHONY COOKBOOK
215 Victoria Street
Toronto, Ontario. M5B 1V1

A fund raising project of the Toronto Symphony Women's Committee

Please send me .... copies of *The Toronto Symphony Cookbook* at $8.95 each, plus $1.00 per book to cover mailing costs.

Enclosed is my cheque or money order for $ . . . . made out to *The Toronto Symphony Cookbook,* or CHARGEX . . . . / . . . . . . / . . . . . . / . . . . . .

Name . . . .

Street . . . .

City . . . . Province . . . .

Postal Code . . . .

All proceeds from the sale of these cookbooks are for the benefit of The Toronto Symphony.